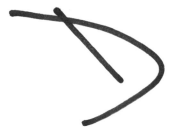

SCIENCE

FOUNDATIONS

Artificial Intelligence

SCIENCE FOUNDATIONS

Artificial Intelligence
Atomic Structure
The Big Bang
Cell Theory
Electricity and Magnetism
Evolution
The Expanding Universe
The Genetic Code
Germ Theory
Global Warming and Climate Change
Gravity
Heredity
Kingdoms of Life
Light and Sound
Matter and Energy
Natural Selection
Planetary Motion
Plate Tectonics
Quantum Theory
Radioactivity
Theory of Relativity
Vaccines
Viruses
The Water Cycle

SCIENCE FOUNDATIONS

Artificial Intelligence

P. ANDREW KARAM

CHELSEA HOUSE

An Infobase Learning Company

Chelsea House
An imprint of Infobase Learning
132 West 31st Street
New York, NY 10001

Library of Congress Cataloging-in-Publication Data
Karam, P. Andrew.
  Artificial intelligence / by P. Andrew Karam.
      p. cm. — (Science foundations)
  Includes bibliographical references and index.
   ISBN 978-1-61753-027-2 (hardcover : aicd-free paper) 1. Artificial intelligence—Juvenile literature. I. Title. II. Series.
  Q335.4.K37 2011
  006.3—dc23   2011012800

Chelsea House books are available at special discounts when purchased in bulk quantities for businesses, associations, institutions, or sales promotions. Please call our Special Sales Department in New York at (212) 967-8800 or (800) 322-8755.

You can find Chelsea House on the World Wide Web at
http://www.infobaselearning.com

Text design by Kerry Casey
Cover design by Alicia Post
Composition by EJB Publishing Services
Cover printed by Yurchak Printing, Landisville, Pa.
Book printed and bound by Yurchak Printing, Landisville, Pa.

Printed in the United States of America

This book is printed on acid-free paper.

All links and Web addresses were checked and verified to be correct at the time of publication. Because of the dynamic nature of the Web, some addresses and links may have changed since publication and may no longer be valid.

Contents

What Is Artificial Intelligence?

Artificial intelligence (AI) consists of machines that are as smart, or smarter, than humans. Most often, computers control these machines. There are many examples of artificial intelligence in science fiction films and shows. One example is the Cylons in the TV and film franchise *Battlestar Galactica,* which are robots that turned against humans. Other examples include the smart robots and Skynet from the *Terminator* movies and TV series. These machines were examples of evil artificial intelligence that were trying to kill people. If this is what AI research represents, do we really want to make intelligent machines?

On the other hand, everybody who watches *Star Trek* knows that artificial intelligence can be a good thing. The **android** character Lieutenant Commander Data uses his intelligence and strength to help his crewmates. Because of his design, he will not hurt people. If intelligent robots of the future are made like Data, programmed not to harm humans, we should not worry. Instead, we should be developing AI as quickly as possible.

The previous examples make opinions about AI seem simple: If smart robots are evil, then we should not create them; if smart robots are good, then perhaps we should create them. However, nothing is ever that simple. For example, as sci-fi fans know, Data had an evil "brother," and there were a few Cylons and Terminator

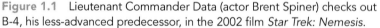

Figure 1.1 Lieutenant Commander Data (actor Brent Spiner) checks out B-4, his less-advanced predecessor, in the 2002 film *Star Trek: Nemesis*.

robots that were good. They were actually helpful to humans. Even in these popular fictional shows and movies, the truth is that intelligent machines were neither completely good nor bad. Today we are unclear as to whether artificial intelligence is going to end up as humanity's savior, destroyer, or simply another tool for us to use. In any case, you need to know the basics about AI before deciding on its pros and cons, so keep reading.

WHAT ARE SENTIENCE AND INTELLIGENCE?

Two key words used a lot in AI research are **sentience** and **intelligence**. The first term, *sentience*, is a little easier to understand.

Sentience is the ability to feel and to experience perceptions—in other words, to experience the world through the senses of sight, hearing, touch, smell, and taste. How can computers or robots be sentient? A computer can be hooked up to a camera or a scanner that feeds images into it the same way that human eyes feed images into the brain. Thus, in this sense, computers can see. Also, we can hook up computers to microphones and even program them to recognize words when a person talks into a microphone or telephone. Therefore, computers can also hear. Incredibly, there are even devices that help computers to smell, taste, and touch, although these are still being developed and perfected. The bottom line is that some computers and robots are able to sense the world. Whether or not they can understand or appreciate what their senses tell them is something else.

Some scientists think that there is more to sentience than just being able to sense the world. They think that to be truly sentient one must be able to experience the sensation in an emotional way. When a dog smells food, it gets excited. When it sees a family member, it becomes happy. These scientists would say that even after attaching a camera to a computer to allow it to see, the computer would not feel excited if its owner walked in front of the lens. There is a difference between a computer "seeing" a scanned image and a dog or a person seeing something that makes them happy. By definition, we might say that a computer is sentient because it can be fitted with cameras, microphones, and other sensors to touch and taste. However, some scientists would still say that just because a computer can sense, it is not necessarily true that it is sentient, or sensitive in perception or feeling.

The other key word in AI research is *intelligence*. It is difficult to precisely define this word. An intelligent person is smart, and intelligence has something to do with the ability to think. A dictionary definition of *intelligence* might say something like, "having the ability to learn new things, to learn from experience, and to use this knowledge to solve problems." Let's try to put this definition to use in AI.

Part of the definition of *intelligence* is about the ability to learn, and most of us would agree that learning means that we are adding new knowledge about something to our brains. When students are young, they learn that 2 + 2 = 4, and they learn that George

Washington was the first U.S. president. Before they learned these facts, they did not know them. Learning these things added knowledge to their brains. So how does that work with a machine? If a person loads his or her computer with the *Encyclopedia Britannica,* has the computer learned everything in the encyclopedia? If so, what happens when that information is deleted? Has the computer now "unlearned," or forgotten, the encyclopedia? Or, is there more to learning than simply adding facts to a person's brain?

Another part of the definition of intelligence is the ability to learn from experience. For example, say a person turns off a light bulb and grabs it right away. After burning his fingers, he learns that this is not a good idea. He might even learn to wait a few minutes to let the light bulb cool off, or to use a towel or washcloth to keep his fingers from burning. The point is that this person learns from the bad experience of grabbing a hot light bulb.

Computers can learn, too. People can take a computer, robot, or any other device that has computer controls and fit it with temperature sensors and a mechanical arm. Then, we can let it grab a number of different objects, programming it to recognize when something is so hot it would hurt a person. We could program it not to pick up the object again in the future. Thus, the experience of picking up a hot light bulb—even if the computer does not feel pain—can still teach it to avoid hot light bulbs in the future. In other words, we can say that the computer has learned from its experience of picking up a hot light bulb. This means that computers can pass two of the tests for intelligence mentioned earlier. However, what about the third test? Can a computer use what it has learned to solve problems?

To some extent, computers can learn to solve problems, depending on the sorts of problems they receive. For example, a computer can use its thermal sensors and programming to solve the simple problem of how long it must wait after turning off a light bulb to safely pick it up. On the other hand, a computer probably cannot fight a war all on its own. That sort of problem is too complicated, since there are too many jobs to do and too many decisions for a computer to make. Computers are even worse at recognizing right from wrong, especially when the issues are not clear-cut. If two people are arguing about who should get a car, a computer might simply decide that each person should get half. Although computers might be able to use their experiences to solve simple problems, they cannot handle the more complicated ones people deal with every day. This does not mean that computers will *never* be able to solve these sorts of hard problems. It just means they can't do it yet.

MAKING MACHINES THAT CAN MAKE "INTELLIGENT" DECISIONS

Part of having intelligence is being able to make decisions. Some easy decisions might include whether or not to go to the restroom, or if it is safe enough to cross the street. People make thousands of decisions every day. In fact, any animal with a brain can make a decision of sorts—depending on how we define the word *decision*. An ant crawling across the ground might run into a stick and be forced to "decide" whether to crawl over it, turn right, or turn left, but an ant's "decisions" are made by following very simple rules that are encoded into its DNA. Thus, an ant might "decide" to turn right when it runs into a stick, but this sort of decision is sort of similar to saying that a ball "decides" to drop when it rolls off the end of a table. The ant has no more choice over which way it turns than a ball has a choice about falling—something instinctive like this is probably not what we think of as being a decision. A dog might be able to choose between a tasty steak and dry dog food, but it can't decide what movie it would like to see on TV. The decisions that people make are more complicated than the ones made by ants or dogs because human lives are more complicated than the lives of animals. The reason that humans can have complicated lives is that our intelligence has enabled us to create a more complicated world.

Before most people make decisions, they consider the pros and cons of their options. Their choices come from *all* of the information available. There are, however, other ways of making decisions that don't require as much thought. One example of this is a decision made several times each day on nuclear submarines. Submarines cannot hear very well what's behind them, so every so often they engage in maneuvers to ensure no one is following them.

There are several ways of finding out what might be behind them, including the use of baffle-clearing patterns. A submarine captain doesn't want to be predictable. If the submarine's actions are expected, an enemy will be able to hunt the vessel. Therefore, the control room of every submarine contains a pair of dice. Every so often, one of the officers will roll the dice two times. The first roll decides when the submarine will conduct its maneuver. The second roll decides the pattern chosen by the captain, who consults a table such as the one shown here. By allowing the dice to make these decisions, the captain knows that his decisions will be purely random. An enemy captain can't predict what will happen or when it will happen.

This is the kind of decision a computer can easily make. The only problem is that it is not an *intelligent* decision. Chance makes the choice, rather than a thinking process. Sometimes random decisions are a good way to go, but they can't be confused with any decision that requires intelligence.

Table 1.1: Submarine "Baffle-clearing" Patterns		
Dice Roll	Time of maneuver	Maneuver to use
1	Between 00 and 05 (on the hour to 5 minutes after the hour)	Pattern 1
2	05-10	
3	10-15	Pattern 2
4	15-20	
5	20-25	Pattern 3
6	25-30	
7	30-35	Pattern 2
8	35-40	
9	40-45	Pattern 1
10	45-50	
11	50-55	Pattern 3
12	55-00	

Table 1.1   This is an example of a table that a submarine captain might use to decide which pattern to adopt when checking to see if he is being followed.

What Is IQ?

For thousands of years, people have recognized that some people are smarter than others. Yet they had trouble measuring this. What was needed was a way to measure intelligence. In 1912, a German psychologist named William Stern was the first to use the term *intelligence quotient*, abbreviated *IQ*. This quotient was thought to be a way to measure a person's intelligence. Two other scientists, Alfred Binet and Theodore Simon, developed the first IQ test. To this day, however, not everyone agrees on what this exam and its results really mean.

At first glance, a person's IQ score is supposed to measure his or her intelligence. A person of average intelligence will have an IQ of 100. A score lower than 100 means an intelligence that is below average. Scores higher than 100 signify an intelligence that is higher than average. This is not a bad assumption. The problem is that measuring human intelligence is a lot more complex than people originally imagined.

Scientists have come to realize that there are many different kinds of intelligence. Some people are good at math, while others excel at writing. There are people who are amazing in music, art, or recognizing patterns. Judging people's intelligence based on how well they do on a math and English test might not be fair if they have stronger abilities in other skills. Thus, giving everyone the same test might not be the best way to determine who is smarter, or who has a higher IQ.

This leads us to an interesting question: If we can't understand how to measure intelligence in people, then how are we going to know how intelligent machines are?

Computers are also good at making simple decisions, similar to the way an ant does. An ant's decisions are rooted in answers embedded in its DNA. Computers can become programmed with rules telling them what to do in common situations. People, on the other hand, do not use simple rulebooks while making decisions. There are many decisions that need more than math or simple rules, such as buying a car. Some people like to buy cars that will impress other people. However, a computer doesn't know that a Mercedes might impress people in one neighborhood, while a Volvo might rank higher in another area. Other people simply fall in love with a certain kind of car and want to buy it for that reason. Computers don't know how to tell the difference between a car that a teen might love and one that a parent might love.

Every day, people decide whether to get married, buy a home, or change to a profession that will make them happier. Some of the most important decisions people make, however, are the most challenging for a computer. Of course, some of these decisions are not easy for people to make either. When people let machines make complicated decisions, the machines often make mistakes. For

How Do We Measure a Machine's Intelligence?

Measuring the intelligence of a machine is more difficult than figuring out the intelligence of a person. We can program a machine to know the answers to almost any factual question. Computers are better than humans at figuring out math problems and memorizing grammar rules. If a teacher gives a computer a math or science test, the computer will look like the smartest "person" taking the exam. However, if the teacher asks a computer to write an essay, it will falter. If the teacher asks it to find symbolism in a painting, it will do worse than most people will.

Many of the intelligence or problem-solving tests that researchers give to people are not good ways to test computers. For example, math problems are used to test human intelligence, but computers can be programmed to do perfectly on math questions. Tests that rely on facts are not helpful in determining if a computer is intelligent, because facts can be loaded into a computer's hard drive. In those sorts of difficult decisions, there is still no substitute for a human mind.

MAKING MACHINES THAT CAN THINK

Computers can become sentient, they can learn, and they can make simple decisions. Yet, in spite of this, computers today are not yet what one would call intelligent. All of this raises a question: How do scientists make a machine that can actually *think*? How do they make a computer that can solve complicated problems that call for more than simple, random chance or simple rules?

In humans, IQ measures intelligence. Human intelligence resides in the brain, which is made of cells called *neurons*. Some computer scientists think that brain cells serve the same function as the

1950, one of the first computer scientists, Alan Turing, determined the best test of a machine's intelligence. The test should not consist of asking a machine to answer specific questions. Rather, a person should try to carry on a conversation with the machine. Turing suggested putting a human judge in a room with two terminals: one with a person on the other end and the other hooked up to a computer. The judge wouldn't know which terminal had the person on the other end and which had the computer. The judge's job was to try to figure out which one was the computer and which was the person. If a computer can fool the judge into thinking it's a person, then the computer is intelligent.

One problem with the Turing test is that we don't know if a computer is really thinking or if it is just very cleverly simulating thought. We can only know what the computer communicates with us. On the other hand, we can say the same thing about everyone around us. When we talk with another person, how can we know what is actually taking place inside his or her head? The Turing test might have some potential problems, but it is still about the best we can do.

transistors on a computer chip. These researchers feel that human intelligence depends both on the number of neurons and on how these cells are connected. The average human brain contains 100 billion neurons. This is 333 times more neurons than there are in a cat's brain, and 1 million to 10 million times more than in an ant's brain.

According to these scientists, the reason humans are intelligent is due to all the neurons in the human brain. They believe computers could become as intelligent as humans are if the function and number of computer chip transistors were the same as brain neurons. One problem with this approach is that examples exist that do not support it. For instance, whales and elephants have twice as many neurons as humans and are very smart. However, research shows they are not as intelligent as humans are. If that's the case, then intelligence must depend on more than just the number of brain cells or the number of transistors. Today's high-performance computers have about a billion transistors per chip. This number is close to the amount of neurons a dog brain has. Yet most people would agree that computers and dogs do not have the same level of intelligence. This suggests that there is more to intelligence than just having the right **hardware**. If scientists are going to try to develop artificial intelligence, then they must figure out how smart a machine is.

Other scientists have pointed out that there is more to our brains than just the number of neurons. Each neuron sends out tens or hundreds of stalks, or *dendrites*, which touch other neurons. With time, these linkages change. For instance, when a person learns something new, his or her neurons rewire themselves to connect differently than they had before learning the new information. The brain is a dynamic network of interconnected cells. Maybe, then, the *complexity* of the brain (the neurons *plus* their connectedness) is what makes people intelligent. If that's the case, scientists need to make a computer that has a huge number of transistors, each of which is connected with tens or hundreds of other transistors on the same computer chip. This has not yet been accomplished.

There are two main schools of thought among AI researchers. One camp believes that intelligence will automatically appear when the hardware becomes complicated enough. A computer will become intelligent when it has as many transistors as a human brain has cells. These transistors must be interconnected, like brain cells. Other scientists argue that this is a little too simple. They think that it will take not only hardware, but also **software**. If this is the case, then the hardware will need to be complex enough to run the program. Yet the programming is what makes the computer intelligent.

The scientists who feel that software is the key to artificial intelligence are trying to write intelligent programs that will help the computer to learn, use what it has learned, and make decisions. In AI research, this is the basic issue that needs to be overcome. Unless scientists can answer this question, the only way they're going to design an intelligent machine is through sheer luck. Today's common belief is that the making of an intelligent machine requires both first-rate hardware and cutting-edge software.

The History of AI

Intelligence is the main trait that makes humans different from animals. It is what lets humans think about the future and plan activities. It gives humans the ability to communicate complex thoughts. It makes it possible to build and use tools and machines. Because of intelligence, humans recognize patterns and all the other things that distinguish their lives. On the whole planet, only humans are intelligent. Yet, in all of human history, there have been tales of people trying to create other forms of intelligence. In the text that follows, we will look at some of the ways in which people have pursued this quest, from ancient times through to the computer age.

It's worth keeping in mind that each generation thinks of the brain in terms of the highest technology present in its civilization. In earlier times, people did not think in terms of computers because computers didn't exist. People had mechanical technology, and so they thought in mechanical terms. They tried their hand at building mechanical creatures that they hoped would be able to work or perform on their behalf.

The highest technology of the current era is the computer. It follows, therefore, that many scientists think of the brain as a sort of living computer. Today, most of the work on artificial intelligence is focused on computer hardware and software. Researchers are trying to make computers that imitate the way the brain works. Hence, much of what follows focuses on advances in computer science and how it has advanced the field of artificial intelligence research. But first, back to the beginning!

EARLY LEGENDS AND FABLES

The Greeks, Egyptians, and Chinese stand out as having the great civilizations of the ancient world. All of these ancient civilizations had myths and stories about what is now called artificial intelligence. However, most of their stories were told in terms of artificial men. Such artificial men are what we would call robots today.

Take ancient Greece, for example. In Greece, Hephaestus, the god of craftsmen and technology, was said to have made himself metal **automatons**. These automatons, including walking tripods, would help him with his work and bring things back and forth from his home to **Mount Olympus**. According to Homer's epic poem *The Iliad,* Hephaestus also created human-like machines made of bronze to help him move from place to place. One of Hephaestus's creations, Talos, was a giant man made of bronze. Talos was responsible for protecting the island of Crete from pirates and other invaders. He would circle the island three times each day to do so. A similar story tells of a sculptor called Pygmalion who falls in love with one of his creations. This creation is brought to life by the goddess Venus.

Then there's the real-life invention of the ancient Greeks that is so complex that, for many decades, scholars had no idea what it was. When they finally figured it out, they were stunned. It seemed that the ancient Greeks invented a mechanical computer about 2,000 years before anyone else even had an idea that such a thing could be done.

Ancient Egypt, like Greece, had its own mythology that included statues that could feel emotion and think. Yet arguably the most interesting tale of artificial intelligence is from ancient China. More than 2,000 years ago, a tale started of a mechanical man made for the emperor by the craftsman Yan Shi. This mechanical man was said to be able to walk and sing. It also winked at the ladies of the royal court, making the emperor jealous. It acted just like a person. In fact, Yan Shi's mechanical man was so lifelike, the emperor wanted to execute him. Yan Shi then proved to the emperor that his mechanical man was an automaton and not a real human being.

The Antikythera Device: A 2,000-year-old Computer?

A little more than a century ago, in the year 1900, some Greek divers were riding out a storm off the island of Antikythera, just north of the Greek island of Crete. They decided to dive for sponges while they were waiting for the storm to pass. Instead, they found an ancient shipwreck that was later dated to about 100 B.C. During the few years that followed, **archeologists** continued diving to explore the wreck. Then, in 1902, Greek archeologist Valerios Stais (1857–1923) found what looked like a gear stuck inside of a rock. Thinking it was part of an ancient clock, he brought it to the surface. Finding an ancient clock would have been amazing because clocks weren't invented until at least 1,000 years after the ship's sinking.

Decades later, in 1959, British historian Derek de Solla Price (1922–1983) realized something new. The device was really a type of computer called an **analog computer**. It had been built to track the planet positions and moon phases. While a clock would have been an amazing discovery, finding a computer from so many years ago was even more awesome. Also amazing was that scientists found hints about similar machines. These machines, now called Antikythera devices (or mechanisms), were from the same time period as the shipwreck. Far from being a unique invention, it is now thought to have been one of many similar devices made by the ancient Greeks.

What is amazing is that it took another 1,500 years for European workers to make something equally as complex. According to an article in one of the world's best scientific journals, *Nature*, the theories about this device might have been developed before the Greeks. The universe that it

A few thousand years later, in the ninth century, the Arab alchemist Jabir ibn Hayyan (721–815) considered how to create artificial life. Four centuries after Jabir, another Arab scientist named al-Jazari

Figure 2.1   A reconstruction of an Antikythera device is shown on display at the Second International Conference on the Ancient Technology in Athens, Greece, in 2005. It consists of at least 29 gears of various sizes that were made to move simultaneously via a handle.

encoded seems to be line with ancient Babylonian thinking. Thus, the computer is not a recent invention. It is one that can be traced back to ancient times.

(1136–1206) created a device he called a peacock fountain. It used mechanical servants to help guests wash their hands. Al-Jazari also made a band of robots that played music.

Figure 2.2 The Golem of Prague, the legendary robot defender of Medieval Jews, stands at the entrance to the former Jewish area in the Czech Republic's largest city.

Jewish legends tell about a late sixteenth–century rabbi, Judah Loew ben Bezalel (1520–1609) of Prague, who made a *golem*—a man made of clay that was brought to life through rituals and magic. According to legend, the Golem of Prague was created to protect the Jews of the city from attack. However, it became more and more violent and could not be controlled. It finally was stopped when the rabbi was able to erase the first letter of a word written on the golem's forehead. The rabbi changed the word from *emet* (Hebrew for "truth") to *met* (Hebrew for "death").

What all these creations had in common was that most of them were automata. Automata were mechanical beings that acted but did not think. Although not an automaton, the golem still was not what would be considered intelligent. Even when the golem started acting on its own, it still was not acting intelligently. It behaved like a chaotic animal. Thus, in these fables, there is a part of, but not all of an artificial intelligence. Described in these tales are artificial beings that can move and act on their own, even if they can't think very well. The addition of thinking machines came later, during the industrial age. This was a time when scientists and philosophers guessed about the mysteries of human thought and how it might be copied.

INDUSTRIAL-AGE ATTEMPTS

After the fall of the Roman Empire, Europe fell into a thousand-year slump. The Middle Ages began, a time when progress almost stopped completely. Knowledge in the form of ancient texts was preserved in Europe by Christian monks and Arab scholars. Europeans added little to the sum of human knowledge for nearly a millennium. This began to change in the fourteenth century with the advent of the **Renaissance**. This was a period of 300 years of intellectual rebirth that started in Tuscany, Italy. During this time, people started to look for reasons behind the existence of what they saw in the world. Following the Renaissance was another period called the **Enlightenment**. This was a period even more focused on using scientific principles to try to understand the world.

In an era when people were trying to find reason in the world around them, many wanted to know how the human mind worked. Since people were trying to explain the planets, Earth, the stars, and the animals, it was natural to try to understand the nature of thought itself. Part of this effort was driven by more subtle motives. If people were using their powers of thought to learn about the world, then maybe they should also try to understand their powers of thought. In other words, the mind is the tool a person uses to understand the world. Renaissance scholars and philosophers simply wanted to feel comfortable that they could trust what the mind was telling them.

By the time the Industrial Age emerged, humans were developing and using machines more and more. During this period, the world saw the development of steam engines, steam ships, and locomotives. Humanity was inventing powered devices that could do much of what humans had done in the past with their own strength. It was only natural to assume that human thought was something like a machine and, thus, machines could be designed that would help do tasks that previously could only be done by people.

With this idea as a backdrop, scientists tried to understand the human mind and recreate it in machinery. In the seventeenth century, French philosopher Rene Descartes (1596–1650) took the first step. He described animals as complex machines that could be understood. He was less certain, however, about what made up human thoughts. Around the same time, in 1623, the German scientist Wilhelm Schickard (1592–1635) built the first mechanical calculating machine. He didn't tell many people about his invention and, after his machine was destroyed in a fire a year after it was made, he gave up on it. We wouldn't know about it at all, except for a few letters he wrote that went unfound for more than three centuries.

During the same time, the English philosopher Thomas Hobbes (1588–1679) was thinking along the same lines as Schickard. He concluded that thinking was like calculating. In his respected work *Leviathan*, he said, "reason is nothing but reckoning." In the seventeenth century, the problem was also approached by the German mathematician and philosopher Gottfried Leibniz (1646–1716). Leibniz invented calculus and a number of different mechanical calculators. In addition, he invented the **binary** number system. This system lies at the heart of nearly every computer and computer language in use today. Most interestingly, Leibniz also tried to develop a "calculus of reason." This type of math was based on his belief that it would be possible to use formulas to represent human thought. Leibniz thought it would be possible to calculate equations applied

Figure 2.3 In the early 1840s, Ada Lovelace translated an article by Italian mathematician Luigi Menabrea on the analytical engine, and added her own notes. The notes contain what is considered to be the first written computer program—an algorithm encoded for processing by a machine.

to basic human problems and thoughts. If Leibniz were correct, then we could easily make machines that could think.

Trying to mechanize thought and build machines to solve math formulas were common goals in the following century. This line of work occupied both inventors and philosophers. It reached a peak in the first half of the nineteenth century, primarily thanks to the work of Charles Babbage (1791–1871) and Countess Ada Lovelace (1815–1852). Babbage, a British mathematician and inventor, created the world's most advanced calculating devices while Lovelace developed the world's first programming language to run them. These were the difference engine and the analytical engine. Once built, the difference engine (later called Difference Engine No. 1) could perform simple calculations. It was also great at cranking out tables of numbers. At that time, "computers" were people who performed computations. Babbage's dream was to save computers from the thankless job of calculating many numbers in long math tables. His device would also reduce the number of human errors in these tables.

Though its design was completed, the creation of Difference Engine No. 2 was not completed in Babbage's lifetime. The technology needed to finish it was not around during that era. Following Babbage's plans, a working model of Difference Engine No. 2 was finally built between 1989 and 1991. Its successful creation proved that the basic design was sound.

Running into snags with the difference engine, Babbage regrouped and then (with Lovelace's help) tried to go far beyond his original plans. They designed a machine that would not only perform calculations, but could also be programmed using punched cards to give instructions to the machine. Using these cards, a programmer could build complex sets of instructions. If fully realized, the analytical engine would have been the same as a basic computer. Key to all of this was Lovelace's work. She was possibly the only person to understand what Babbage was trying to accomplish. She was also the inventor of the world's first programming language. As with the difference engine, the analytical engine was never to be built.

Even so, Babbage and Lovelace were on track to making a full-blown computer. In theory, this would have been similar to those being used today. It's tempting to wonder how the world might be different today, had they been successful then: The field of artificial intelligence might well have been advanced by at least a century. In

Figure 2.4 Charles Babbage first conceived the idea of an advanced calculating machine to calculate and print mathematical tables in 1812, as a way to eliminate inaccuracies associated with compiling mathematical tables by hand. Difference Engine No. 1 (*above*) was begun in 1824 and assembled in 1832 by Joseph Clement, a skilled toolmaker and draughtsman. It was a decimal digital machine—the value of a number represented by the positions of toothed wheels marked with decimal numbers.

addition, the first computer would have been powered by steam, and the first programs would have churned their way through wooden and metal gears, instead of electronic components. Instead, the first real computer had to wait for the arrival of the early electronic age.

Before leaving the Victorian Age, it should also be noted that other thinkers had their opinions about the field. British writer Samuel Butler (1835–1902) was the first person to consider that, like animals, machines might evolve. If so, he thought they might someday become smart enough to replace humans.

EARLY COMPUTER-AGE RESEARCH

Babbage died in 1871. After his death, work on computing machines stopped for more than 50 years. Then, in 1941, German engineer Konrad Zuse (1910–1995) invented the first operational and programmable computer. However, Zuse ran into some of the same snags that had caused problems for Babbage. In 1936, Zuse was trying to make a computer with mechanical pieces. Like Babbage, he found that the technology of his day was not up to the challenge. But Zuse kept trying, and within five years was finally able to get the Z3 working.

Instead of **vacuum tubes**, the machine used **electromechanical** telephone parts. Vacuum tubes were invented in 1906, but were not widely used at first. In fact, the German military didn't see the sense in trying to upgrade the Z3 to electronics. Instead, Zuse was put to work making computers that could help design new weapons. Zuse was mostly interested in designing computers for practical purposes anyway. Since Germany was in the middle of World War II, he wanted to help with that effort more than with advancing computer design.

During wartime, on the other side of the English Channel, a British mathematician was busy at work. Alan Turing (1912–1954) was building his own electromechanical computer. It was designed to help break the secret code the Germans were using. The computer he helped design and program was important in helping the Allies win the war. Yet it could be argued that his work in the field of artificial intelligence was even more important than his wartime work.

Turing was the first to come up with the idea of what is now called the **Turing test**. This is a way to decide if a computer is actually

Figure 2.5 British mathematician Alan Turing came up with the Turing test so humans could test a machine's ability to exhibit intelligent behavior.

The Turing Test

Alan Turing found a way to check for a computer's intelligence. A person could communicate through a terminal and guess whether there was a computer or human on the other end. If the person could not tell the difference between a computer and human, then the computer was said to be intelligent. Today, **digital computers** are most often used for these tests.

Turing felt that digital computers could do whatever was asked of them. They could even pass the Turing test, if given enough memory, computing speed, and time. But even though Turing and researchers since his time have felt that computers will one day become truly smart, others have disagreed. These scientists have felt that no matter how powerful and how well it is programmed, a machine can never be truly intelligent.

Some critics have said that intelligence is part of the human soul, and since we can't give souls to machines, we can't make an intelligent computer. Turing's reply was that designing intelligent machines was no different than creating children because, in his opinion, humans in both cases

intelligent. He also came up with the idea of the **Turing machine**. Simply put, this is a machine that will follow a set of instructions according to a particular set of rules. The set of instructions is very similar to what is now called a computer program. This was a new concept in the 1940s, but today just about everybody has a "Turing machine" at home: a computer. The user enters the computer's instructions in the form of a program. Then, the computer follows the instructions according to the rules of its operating system. Turing was the first person to explain the theory behind this whole process.

After Turing, progress in the field of artificial intelligence picked up speed. These advances can be generally divided into one of three categories:

1. *Hardware*: Engineers worked to develop newer and more powerful computers.

would be acting as instruments of God's will. Another objection is that computers will never be intelligent because they can never have emotions. Turing replied that we have no way of knowing whether any other human really feels emotions the same way that we do. We just assume they do. Thinking the same way, Turing said we shouldn't waste time by worrying or wondering whether computers are either feeling or faking emotions. If a computer acts intelligent, it doesn't matter.

One of the oldest objections about computers being able to be intelligent dates back to the time of Countess Ada Lovelace. The argument is that computers can't be original, since they can't come up with new ideas. Turing felt that enough computing speed and memory helps a computer analyze complex problems. Their answers would even surprise humans. This would show that computers have the ability to be original.

Turing responded to every objection that was brought up, giving his answers for why we should be able to develop intelligent computers. In the time since Turing's death, the debate hasn't changed very much. Turing's answers seem just as relevant today as they were in 1950.

2. **Software**: Programmers worked to develop new and more powerful programming languages, operating systems, and programs.
3. **Wetware**: Mathematicians, cognitive scientists, and philosophers worked to develop better theories of how human minds and thoughts work.

For many years, there has been a huge debate over whether or not computers could ever really think. As one example, the pioneering computer scientist and mathematician John von Neumann (1903–1957) gave a lecture in 1949 about computer intelligence. At that time, someone in the audience said that it would be impossible for a computer to think. Von Neumann replied, "If you will tell me precisely what it is that a machine cannot do, then I can always make a machine which will do just that." What von Neumann meant was that he could program a computer to do any specific activity. For example, a programmer can make a computer say, "Hello, how are you?" each time it meets somebody for the first time. A computer can also be programmed to follow any other rule. If we come up with a list of actions we think are marks of intelligence, we can program a computer to follow them. This is a software approach to creating intelligent computers. It assumes that smart programming is all it takes to create artificial intelligence.

Hardware researchers take a different approach. They trust technology to make a machine that is genuinely intelligent. They think that artificial intelligence depends on a computer's speed and processor connections. They also think it depends on memory, the right type of software, or a combination of both. In their view, intelligence will show up on its own when a computer is as complex as a human brain.

Both the hardware and software groups make use of the advances of the wetware scientists. These are the scientists who come up with **hypotheses** about how the brain works and puts thoughts together. One wetware scientist might study how neurons are linked together. Then, a computer engineer would try to build a computer wired together in the same manner. Still another wetware scientist might develop a theory about how neurons communicate with each other, helping humans make decisions. A software engineer would then try to write a program to mimic that process. The work of the wetware scientists supports both of these groups. Without the basic understanding of how the brain and the mind work, it is hard to develop the hardware and software to imitate it.

UNDERSTANDING HUMAN THOUGHT

Since the 1970s scientists have worked hard in all of these areas. They have tried to develop powerful computers and advanced running software. Their goal: to create a genuinely intelligent machine. The problem is that original human thought is still too complex to completely understand. By the 1970s, some researchers were talking about bringing together aspects of human intelligence. Their interest was not in making a computer that could talk with humans. Rather, they wanted to design a program that could imitate human thought in very specific areas. These areas are called *expert systems.*

An expert system is a computer program designed to put into code the same level of knowledge that a human expert would have in his or her subject area. It also follows the same rules a human uses to make decisions. For example, there are expert systems that are used to evaluate EKGs, the electrical patterns coming from the human heart. These signals determine if a person's heart is healthy. In most cases, studies have shown that computer systems are just as good at diagnosing heart problems as human doctors are. The reason for this is that the programmers can interview hundreds or thousands of medical experts. They ask each doctor how he or she goes about making decisions and doing his or her job. With this information, programmers can start to develop rules for how experts evaluate data and situations. Those rules can be programmed into computers.

In many cases, a well-programmed computer can make decisions that are as good as those a human can make. Unlike humans, computers can be trusted to evaluate the same data the same way, every time, regardless of how long they've been working. Simply stated, computers don't get tired. Therefore, in some targeted areas, these expert systems seem to be about as smart as humans.

It's worth going through an example of how this process works. Say you're babysitting and you hear a strange noise. What goes through your mind? There are several possibilities. Maybe somebody is trying to break into the house! It could be that the child is stuck in a closet or one of the rooms of the house. Or he may have fallen down and hurt himself. It's also possible that a branch or a tree fell down, that a pet knocked something off a shelf, or that there was a traffic accident in the street outside the house. There are all sorts of things that can cause a strange sound, so you need to try to figure out what sort of sound you heard. Was it the sound of something breaking, something crashing, someone knocking, or someone pounding? What do you do? Do you call the parents, the police, an ambulance, or nobody at all?

Once you identify the type of sound that you hear, you'll be able to take the next step. So say the sound you heard was a crash. The next question is whether the crash came from inside or outside the house. If it was inside, the child might be hurt or might have broken something, or a pet might have caused a problem. If it was outside, it could be a car crash, a tree falling down, somebody trying to break into the house, or something falling off the house. The next question to answer is where the sound was—inside or outside?

Say that now you think that the sound was from inside the house. You've narrowed down the possibilities quite a bit already, but you still don't know if there's a problem. If, for example, the child fell down, he could be hurt and you might have to call the parents or even an ambulance. On the other hand, if a pet knocked something over on a shelf, then you might just have to explain to the parents what happened. So you might listen for what else you hear. If you hear the child crying, then you'd think that he is the cause of the crash, and that he might be hurt. If you hear the pet running away, then you might think that the pet caused the crash. Once you find out exactly what caused the crash from inside the house, you'll know what you should do.

Think about how you could program a computer to deal with the same situation. You'll probably give it a number of questions to try to answer and, depending on the answer to each question, you'll tell the computer what to do or what to ask next. This is called a **decision tree** and it is at the heart of expert systems. A decision tree for the "strange noise while I'm babysitting" scenario might go something like this:

I hear a strange noise.

1. Is the noise a crash, a break, a knock, or a pounding noise?
2. The noise is a crash. Is it from inside or outside the house?
3. The noise is from inside. Do I hear any other noises?
4. I hear a pet running away and I do not hear the child crying.
5. Therefore, the noise was probably the pet knocking over some furniture, and the child is probably okay.

All of this can be programmed into a computer so that a computer can run through the same questions. For each question, the computer can also be programmed to find the answer. With that answer, it knows what to do next. For example, you could put microphones inside and outside the house to help the computer determine the source of a sound. You can also program a computer to "listen" to the microphones and to tell the difference between a knock, a crash, a breaking sound, and a pounding noise. With proper programming, a computer can find the answer to each question as it surfaces. Then, with each answer, it can be programmed to ask and find an answer to the next question.

The computer can also be programmed to call for help when it can't find an answer or when the information it finds is cause for alarm. For example, if the computer identifies the sound as a crash and it hears the child crying, it can be programmed to call for help. It assumes that the child is hurt. It can also be programmed to call the police if it concludes that it has detected a burglar, or to call the parents if the sound is identified as a tree falling on the house. This type of programming, which could include many other types of scenes, would be a sort of babysitting expert system.

Expert systems can be designed to handle almost any situation like this. They can be used where there is a limited number of issues that can come up and where the questions can be resolved by going through a decision tree. Still, we wouldn't consider these computers to be intelligent. There is much more to intelligence than just following a simple set of rules to make decisions. Even though they seem intelligent in some areas, computers are very limited. A computer is like an athlete who might excel in football but can't play basketball or baseball very well. This means that a computer program might be able to look at an EKG and determine if a person has had heart damage, but it might not be able to see a broken bone on an X-ray. In this way, computers are more limited than humans.

Think of typical adults, for example. Chances are that in addition to their jobs, they can write letters, cook meals, and clean the house without breaking things. They can walk through crowded rooms without falling or running into things, and they can carry on conversations. They can play sports (even if they don't play them very well), and so forth. A typical adult might not be as good as a professional at any single thing, but they can do a far greater variety of things than any computer can do.

Something else that computers can't do very well is deal with questions that don't have simple answers. For example, a computer can easily deal with yes or no questions such as, "Is the noise inside the house?" However, they aren't as good at answering unclear questions such as, "Is the child calling for help because he's hurt or because he's joking?" Computers are also bad at making decisions that aren't expressed by numbers. For example, a computer probably can't give its opinion as to which painting in a gallery is most beautiful. It can't say whether a hamburger tastes better or worse than broccoli. It won't tell which song it likes the best. All of these are questions humans can answer.

Then there are questions that are difficult even for humans to answer, regarding topics of right and wrong. As an example, we know that stealing is against the law. We can program a computer to decide that it's never okay to steal. We can also program computers to decide that it's never okay to let someone suffer. But what if someone is suffering from hunger and doesn't have any money? Is it okay for that person to steal food so that he or she doesn't starve to death? Most people would be able to come up with an answer for this question, but a computer might not be able to answer it at all. It might see two things that are wrong, and not be able to see that one might be more wrong than the other one.

For a computer to become intelligent, researchers must find a way to teach it to answer these more difficult questions. These questions don't necessarily have easy, yes or no answers, and they can't be reduced to numbers. So far, such questions are the ones humans are uniquely able to answer. For computers to answer them, programmers will have to find a way to tell them how to think the way humans do.

Problems and Pitfalls
in Developing AI

Artificial intelligence research has progressed significantly since the last years of the twentieth century. Computers today are more powerful than they were in the past, and their software is more complex. Still, although technology is more advanced, artificial intelligence knowledge seems the same as it was a few decades ago. As technology grows, appreciation of the field's challenges grows, too.

One problem is that both the brain and the way it handles information is more complex than earlier imagined. Scientists have known for decades that each neuron has connections to tens or even hundreds of other neurons. However, it was not until recently that researchers learned this network of connections is constantly changing. The changes occur as humans gain new information or experiences. Scientists are also still trying to understand what it is about the brain that lets people feel emotions. What is it about the brain that helps us recognize a face, even when it's half-hidden by a beard? What helps us to find a new way to solve an old problem? What makes it possible to write and appreciate beautiful music? In spite of more than a century of research, much of the way that the brain works is still a mystery. Until researchers really understand all of this, it will be hard to recreate a human brain in hardware and software.

SPEECH AND SPEECH RECOGNITION

Many animals communicate with each other. There are many examples of this in the animal kingdom. Dogs bark to each other. Birds and rodents make alarm sounds when they see predators. There is, however, a difference between communication and language. A mouse squeak that means, "There's a predator—hide!" is not the same as having a conversation about football with your friends. Although animals communicate, as far as is known, only humans have language. Unless a computer or other machine can learn to carry on a conversation, it can't really be considered intelligent. (Remember: This is part of the Turing test.) It is possible to type commands into a keyboard, but it would be easier if we could talk to an intelligent computer or robot the same way that we'd talk to another person. Today's research focuses on getting computers to recognize and understand human speech.

Consider the example of a computerized phone system: We go through all sorts of menus to finally get the information we need, or to speak with a person. Many of these systems use voice recognition. We speak into the phone and the computer on the other end seems to understand what we say. For example, we can speak a number into the phone or say "yes" or "no" and the computer makes the correct response. Speech recognition programs are also available that let us speak into a microphone to make a computer follow our commands or create the text of what we say. The sounds a person makes are changed into electrical impulses, and these in turn prompt commands in the computer. With all of this, it seems as though computers have mastered speech recognition and that we have nothing left to develop. This is far from the truth. Speech recognition is not a done deal. It works well under very controlled conditions (reading numbers or giving simple answers), but in the much more complicated world of following a conversation, speech recognition still has a long way to go.

One thing that makes speech recognition a challenge is that people say words differently. Every pronunciation can sound like a different word to the computer. A computer will do *exactly* what we tell it to do, no more and no less. Even if a computer is programmed to recognize the word *either*, it might not recognize the way a particular person pronounces it. Some people say "ee-ther" and others say "eye-ther." For a computer to recognize a single word, it has to be programmed to understand all of the different ways that people might pronounce it. A computer must be programmed to recognize a New York accent, a Georgia accent, a stuffy nose, a pronunciation mistake, or a little hiccup in the middle of a word. Just to recognize the sound of speaking the numbers zero to nine, a computer might have to be programmed to understand a hundred or more variations. The same can be said of any other batch of individual words. This is why many computer telephone systems stick with very simple lists of single words or numbers and yes and no questions.

There are even more problems that come up when trying to understand the spoken word, at least for computers. Think of all the ways that people speak when they're in a hurry or when they're talking to friends. "Yes" might turn into "yeah" or "yep," or maybe "sure thing" or "you bet." The computer would need to insist that everybody say the one word it is programmed to recognize. Or, the poor programmer has to think of all the different ways that people might say "yes" or "no" or whatever one-word answer is given.

When one thinks of all the ways people can say and pronounce the simplest words, it's a wonder that computers can understand anything at all. Besides that, this level of speech recognition still isn't really artificial intelligence. It's just programming a computer to recognize a specific pattern of sounds as a word, instead of recognizing the letters that a person types. To a computer, understanding the sound "yes" is the same as understanding the typed letters Y-E-S. It is also the same as when a computer user clicks a box marked "yes."

For most people, understanding speech is more than recognizing individual words. It means understanding sentences and paragraphs as they are spoken. This is even more difficult than recognizing individual words. In addition to all the different ways that words can be pronounced, stringing them together into sentences makes things even harder for the computer. When people talk in sentences, they tend to run words together, shorten words, and use contractions. For a computer to recognize speech, it has to be programmed to understand that "can't" means the same as "cannot" and that "didja" means the same as "did you." In addition, there are all the different ways people can put sentences together that all mean pretty much the same thing: for instance, "What time is it?" versus "Hey buddy, you got the time?" and the other stray sounds that find their way into speech ("um" or "uh," for example). Therefore researchers must program a computer to understand that the sound *um* is meaningless when it's a separate word, but that it can also be part of the word *gum* or *bum*.

The next issue might be the hardest to program into a computer. People tend to run their words together when they talk. We hear the individual words because we understand the language and the way it sounds. If you listen to most people when they're talking, you'll notice that the words normally come out without much in the way of gaps between them. We don't say, "Hi. How. Are. You?" when we talk to other people. It comes out more like, "Hi, howareya?"

For a computer to understand what people are saying, it has to figure out where one word ends and the next begins. This isn't impossible. There are software programs that can take what a person says and turn the speech into text. These programs work best when each person "trains" the software to recognize his or her individual speech. This is a process that can take many minutes of speaking to the computer until it can recognize the peculiarities of each person's speech. This works when a person has the time and desire to work for a while with the computer. It won't work with, for example, an artificial intelligence computer that's designed to talk with hundreds or thousands of people every day. For a system that will really understand natural speech—the way people normally talk to each other—a computer has to be able to quickly sort out all of these matters.

As of today, this is not possible. It's a problem that has to be solved if we're going to be able to speak directly to intelligent computers someday. Speech recognition is one of the obstacles of artificial intelligence research. There are others, as well. The following sections will cover other issues that cause problems for artificial intelligence researchers.

CREATIVITY

Creativity is another of the characteristics that seems to make humans unique. Creativity is often thought of as writing novels, composing music, and taking part in other artistic activities, but there is much more to creativity than this. Using a hammer as a paperweight or to prop open a door is a creative act. This is because the person who does this realizes that he can use this tool for something other than the way it is usually used. The ability to be innovative and come up with new ideas is, as far as we can tell, something that not many animals can do, and non-human animals exhibit much less creativity than humans do (for example, a gorilla might realize it can use a twig to get termites out of a termite mound but it can't develop a new theory in physics or compose music). It is also something that we will have to figure out how to program our computers to do if they are going to be genuinely intelligent.

Before discussing creativity in machines, it is necessary to discuss more completely its meaning in humans. One of the challenges to understanding creativity is that it is shown in many different ways. Writers, painters, composers, and scientists will sometimes struggle for months or years, trying to get past a sticking point in their projects. Sometimes they solve their problems one step at a time, like building a house one brick at a time. At other times, inspiration strikes and a person can leapfrog to a solution in a moment. One example of the latter is the story of English physicist and mathematician Isaac Newton (1643–1727) and an apple falling from a tree. Soon after, Newton made a creative leap that helped him understand an important aspect of how gravity works. No matter how it happens, the creative process involves coming up with a new idea. This new idea can be using a hammer to keep papers from blowing away, or realizing that an apple pulls on Earth the same way that Earth pulls on an apple.

The key word here is *new* idea, because coming up with something new is the main problem computers have. We can program computers to follow a set of rules. Yet creativity often involves developing new rules or breaking some of the rules we've learned—for example, using a hammer as a paperweight breaks the "rule" that hammers are used to hit nails.

This is a problem. If computers only know how to follow the rules that we give them, is it possible for these rules to include instructions on when it's okay to break the rules? Although confusing, it is a question that is at the heart of this aspect of artificial intelligence research. We can't tell a computer that it's okay to break every rule. We also can't tell a computer that it's never okay to break a rule. Creativity is being able to understand *which* rules need to be broken to solve a problem. Breaking rules might help a person to develop a new scientific theory or to compose an original piece of music. Creativity also involves knowing *how* to break the rules in a way that helps to solve the problem.

There are different ways programmers work on this problem. One way is to program the computer to make minor, random changes to its program and to see if these small changes make the program better or worse when the computer tries to solve a problem. This is how evolution works. Mutations are minor changes in the information encoded in our DNA. Most of the time these changes are harmful or they have no effect at all. A small fraction of the time, they produce an improvement. The case is the same for the rules programmed into a computer: If the computer makes very small changes at random, most changes will have no effect, or they might even keep the program from running at all. Every once in a while, however, slight changes pave the way for answers.

Let's use the example of a hammer once again. Suppose the computer is loaded with the rule "hammers are used to hit things." Now suppose that, at random, the computer changes *hit* to *hold*, so this rule changes to "hammers are used to hold things." With this small change to one of possibly hundreds of thousands of rules programmed into it, the computer suddenly has a rule that will make it possible to use a hammer as a paperweight. (The purpose of a paperweight is to hold papers in place or to be used as a doorstop, which holds open a door.) Adding one rule—that a computer should make small, random changes to its set of other rules—makes it possible for a computer to be creative . . . at least up to a point.

This sort of experimenting on the part of the computer can be very useful. However, there are two problems present. One is that the computer needs to have a way to know which changes are actually useful and when they can be used. Also, if a computer is making changes at random, there's no guarantee that the changes will go in the direction of a solution to a particular problem. It might, of course, get to an answer by sheer luck.

It is possible to use this process in a more purposeful way. After each random change, the computer could evaluate whether it's closer to a solution than it was before. If the change brings the computer closer to a solution, then the computer can concentrate its next changes in the same direction. By doing this, a computer could work towards a solution to a problem in much the same way as a person would work.

Figure 3.1   This computer-generated art was created based on a mathematical function called the Mandelbrot set, which was created by a human.

These two approaches are similar to how people solve problems. The random changes in computer programs are like flashes of insight. The more directed approach is similar to how a person works steadily towards an answer. The important thing with both of these approaches is to make sure the computer can recognize when it has reached an answer.

There is one sort of creativity that helps people solve problems or recognize other ways of using tools and objects. There is another, more common definition for creativity: writing stories, composing music, creating art, and other artistic activities. Computers can be programmed to do all of these things. So far, though, computer-generated art and music are more successful than computer-generated writing. There are some general rules for both music and art: which colors and shapes go together, which musical notes sound okay together, and so forth. There is still, however, a lot of room for flexibility in these rules.

Think of all of the different types of music—jazz, rock, classical, pop, rap, and more—and think of all the different styles within each of these genres. With art, look at the differences within a group of paintings. There is an infinite number of ways to put together a painting or song that will please an audience. We can program a computer with a set of rules for painting. We can also program it to choose colors and shapes at random, while following rules of composition and color matching. So far, however, computer-generated art and music at their best are okay. Computer-generated masterpieces have not yet been created.

Writing, on the other hand, seems to be a little harder to program. There are all sorts of rules for writing that can be programmed into a computer. There are rules for grammar, vocabulary, sentence structure, and more. What's difficult is to come up with a set of rules for how to make believable characters, place them in believable situations, and tell a story that readers can enjoy. Computers can follow grammar rules, but creating realistic characters who interact with each other and with situations in a believable way calls for an understanding of how people think and behave. This is something that computers can't yet do on their own, although there are some computer programs that can help to write books by providing the outlines of basic sentences, paragraphs, and plot points. These programs can help a person put together a book, but the creativity and the character development—making the characters come across as human—still have to come from the human author. In other words, to date, computer-generated writing is not very good.

Taking all of this into consideration, computers do show some signs of creativity. However, this creativity isn't yet up to human standards. Right now, researchers are not sure if the solution to the problem is faster computing, better programming, or something else. Is creativity a matter of power and programming? Is there a creative spark that only intelligence can have? For the moment, we don't know, but artificial intelligence scientists are working to find answers.

There is one last thing to mention before moving on. There is a difference between breaking rules in the way we're discussing here, and breaking rules that parents, lawyers, or teachers have set. One part of creativity is the breaking of what are called *conceptual* rules. These are the rules about how we view the world. Such rules are different from the ones that help keep us safe and allow us to live as members of society. Researchers are trying to teach computers to be able to break conceptual rules. For example, the rule that "hammers are only used to hit things" may not be programmed into code so that a computer can think of a hammer as a paperweight or a doorstop. Researchers are *not* trying to teach computers to break the rules that say it's bad to steal from others, or that bedtime is at 10 P.M.

ARTIFICIAL SENSES

Yet another problem for the AI researcher is the problem of senses. It is possible to hook up a computer with cameras and microphones that help it to "see" and "hear." They can also be connected to sensors that give them a sense of touch. Robot hands can pick up an egg without breaking it. With **tactile** sensors, a computer can tell if an object is hard or soft, rough or smooth, fragile or sturdy. In fact, engineers have even come up with mechanisms that can tell the difference between different molecules that are floating in the air or are dissolved in water. Artificial taste and robot "noses" are being used to search for explosives, toxins, and other dangers.

People understand the world in which they live thanks to their senses. Try to imagine what life would be like if we couldn't see,

Figure 3.2   A BabyBot robot hand grasps a ball. The BabyBot is a humanoid robot that has been developed at the LIRA-Lab at the University of Genoa in Italy. The BabyBot project, started in 1996, is investigating sensory and control systems, how they interact, and what this can tell us about human brains and how they develop. The hand has five fingers, fifteen joints, and tactile sensors that react by producing a "grasp reflex." Touching one of these sensors (seen under ball) makes the hand close in a grasp, as seen here.

hear, smell, taste, or feel anything. It's almost impossible to think of any creature that can be intelligent without having some way to sense the world around it.

We can give senses to machines so that they can relate to the world around them. The next question is what they can be programmed to do with that information. There are robots that use their senses to hold parts together with just the right amount of pressure during the assembly of a machine. These robots can also use cameras to help them see what they are holding. Another kind of robot, called RABiT, uses cameras and manipulators to analyze laboratory samples. RABiT's analysis helps with research in medical and biological laboratories around the world. Then, of course, there are the speech recognition systems that were mentioned earlier, which use microphones as "ears." With proper programming, these can be used to recognize any sounds, not just speech.

We can give our machines ways to sense the world around them. We can even program computers to make some sense of what

Figure 3.3   A researcher uses a Rapid Automated Bacterial Impedance Technology (RABiT) machine, which is an automated device for measuring the number of microbes in a culture. He is moving a sample that contains microbes into one of the machine's tubes. The tube can be kept at a constant temperature while the microbes multiply by feeding on a nutrient gel. The growth of any microbe colonies can be monitored over time and the results displayed as a graph on a computer screen.

The Challenge of Artificial Vision

For more than a century, cameras have existed to capture images. Yet artificial vision is still an elusive goal. The reason for this is that there is a difference between capturing an image and using that image. Any camera, or eye, can capture an image. However, until that image is interpreted by a mind (or software), it is only an image. The difference between imaging and artificial vision is that vision includes understanding what we've seen. It also includes being able to make use of the image in some way. Facial recognition is one of the ways that artificial vision is being used now. It captures almost all of the challenges of computer vision.

Say, for example, we're trying to program a computer to recognize faces. A digital camera can capture images. Even a simple digital camera can figure out which part of the image is a face. Yet, at first glance, many faces are relatively alike. Most people have the same number of eyes, noses, mouths, and ears arranged in the same pattern. Most of us have hair on the top of our heads. Some of our features might really stand out, such as baldness or having a beard. Still, many of the characteristics that help

their senses are relaying to them. But can we say that computers are actually hearing, seeing, feeling, smelling, and tasting? Or are they simply receiving digital data—the same as when we click on a box for "yes"—without understanding anything of what their senses are receiving?

On the other hand, we can say the same about us: Our eyes, ears, fingers, noses, and tongues produce electrical signals that are sent to the brain in the same way as artificial sensors send electrical signals to a computer. Our brains take these electrical impulses and turn them into images, smells, and other sensory information. Then, our brains turn these impulses into information that means something to us. Is what our brains do with the impulses from our eyes any different from what a computer does with the impulses from a camera? Or maybe a different way to think of it is to ask if *sight* means us to tell the difference between faces are minor: the color of our eyes, the exact shape of a nose and mouth, how far our ears stick out from our heads. It's the sum of all of these minor differences that helps us to tell the difference between faces.

This raises a problem for computers. How can a computer recognize these differences, especially when some things about our faces can change? For instance, we can cut our hair, grow or shave a beard, use colored contact lenses, or wear lipstick. So with all that can change, how do we decide what makes a face recognizable as, say, your sister instead of her best friend?

One way to do this is to program computers to recognize characteristics that don't change. These characteristics might include the exact shape of a person's eye sockets and chin, the distance between their eyes, and so on. Facial recognition software has been used by law enforcement in London and by the U.S. State Department. It has even been used in a few nations to stop voting violations during elections. With good visual conditions, the most recent systems are even able to tell the difference between identical twins.

receiving the images or understanding what they mean. Does this happen in the eye and brain, or in the mind? A computer might receive an image from a camera, if seeing is something that happens in the mind. However, unless it's programmed to understand that image, it is not really seeing. The same can be said of any of the other senses. The body (our "hardware") collects and transmits the information and the mind (our "software") makes sense of it.

When we think about it, we can ask this same question about animals as well. Most animals—even the simplest—have sight, among other senses. The simplest eyes can only tell the difference between light and dark, enough to tell if a possible predator is looming overhead. These are the eyes of a scallop or some worms. But these creatures have virtually no brain and they certainly can't think about what they are seeing. So, does a scallop really "see" the same way that we do? Most of us would say that a scallop is seeing, even without a mind.

What about a computer that's as complex as a scallop's brain and is hooked up to a camera? How complicated does a computer have to be in order for us to say that it can see, hear, taste, smell, and touch? This is a hard question to answer. We don't have a good answer yet. Our ability to create senses for machines has grown faster than our understanding of what happens inside those machines.

THE ABILITY TO MAKE DECISIONS

Another part of being intelligent is being able to make decisions. Some decisions are easy—for example, whether it's safe to cross the street. Easy decisions are ones in which the stakes aren't very high, the questions are not complicated, and there is plenty of information available. This is why crossing the street is an easy decision. We can look in both directions to see if there are any cars coming, we can see how wide the street is, we know how quickly we can walk or run, and so forth. Of course, the stakes can be high. If we don't make it across the street safely, we can be hurt or killed. But, for the most part, deciding whether to cross the street is a relatively easy decision and one that a computer can be programmed to make.

Teaching a machine to make simple decisions is a matter of coming up with rules to follow that will lead to a correct decision. For street crossing, the decision-making program might be something like this:

1. Rule: I can cross the entire street in 10 seconds.
2. Rule: The speed limit on this street is 30 miles per hour (48 kilometers per hour).
3. Rule: Cars moving at 30 miles per hour travel 440 feet in 10 seconds.
4. Rule: Look to the left and then to the right.
5. Question: Do you see any moving cars? If no, make a decision to cross the street. If yes, go to number 6.
6. Question: Does the car look like it's more than 440 feet away? If yes, make a decision to cross the street. If no, make a decision to wait until the car goes by and the street is clear before crossing.

Making a decision about whether or not it's safe to cross a street is therefore simple. There aren't many factors to consider and it's often possible to have all of the information that we need. Yet, even crossing the street is not necessarily as easy as it seems. How does this affect a computer's ability to make this decision? As an example, what if you can't see 440 feet down a street because of a curve or something else that blocks your view? Or what if you don't know whether the cars are moving at the speed limit? Will you have good traction on the road, or might you slip and fall in front of the car?

These are all issues that can make your decision more difficult, and it might be that not all of this information is available the moment you're trying to decide if you can cross safely. If a computer can't see 440 feet (134 meters) away, it might be hit trying to cross when a car is just out of sight. Or it might wait forever to cross since it can't see if there's a car 440 feet down the road or not. Or, for that matter, what about a car that's only 300 feet (91 m) away but moving only 20 miles (32 km) per hour? Either way, the rules listed earlier can't help a computer cross the street.

By the same logic, unless we tell it to do so, a computer won't look at the road to see if it will have good traction. In fact, a computerized system won't look at *anything* that we don't first instruct it to observe. Computers will follow the directions we give them, but they can't go beyond these directions. We can program a computer to cross safely at any specific location. Yet, unless we can think of every single thing that might matter in the decision, we can't program a computer to make a good choice.

It's clear that computers can't always make simple decisions. This suggests that computers might not be able to make some more complicated decisions, either. We will need to come up with complex rules that cover all possible circumstances. We will also need to come up with a way to help computers compensate for missing information and confusing circumstances. This is the sort of thing we do all the time, but computers have problems with it.

Fuzzy logic is a branch of research that studies how to make decisions when we don't have all of the information we need. Instead of using firm answers such as *yes* and *no*, fuzzy logic can find ways to deal with *maybe* and *sort of*. Going back to the street-crossing problem, maybe we can't see the full 440 feet to know whether it's safe to cross the street. However, we can program the computer to make an educated guess as to the chance that a car will be close enough to hit us.

Say, for example, we can see 200 feet (60 m) down the road, leaving 240 feet (73 m) that we can't see. If we see that cars come down the road an average of once each minute, we can calculate the chance a car will be on that important 240 feet of road that we can't see. This is the same stretch of 240 feet where a car might be driving. When it takes a car only 5 seconds to travel that length of road, there are 5 chances in 60 (or 1 chance in 12) that a car won't be seen, but will be close enough to hit us at any point in time. Using fuzzy logic, we can tell the computer, "If you don't see a car, there is a 1 in 12 chance that if you cross the road you'll be run over." We can also

How Computers Hear and Talk

Computer hearing is a lot like computer vision. Microphones can capture sounds and convert them into electrical impulses. However, these impulses must be interpreted before it can be said that the computer hears. Here's how that happens.

Microphones transform sound into electrical impulses. Every word is a group of sounds and each sound makes a very specific shape when examined electronically. A computer can use these patterns to recognize the word that was spoken.

A computer can reverse this process in order to speak. It can select the correct word or sentence based on its programming. It then looks up the correct electrical pattern that when fed into a speaker will create the word it wants. Computerized speech is not always pretty. We can nearly always tell when a computer is talking to us, but it's getting closer to sounding like a person all the time.

program the computer to determine an acceptable level of risk. If we tell the computer that we're willing to take a chance when the risk is less than 50%, the computer will decide to cross the road when it doesn't see a car. This will happen even though, in theory, it will be run over once every 12 times it crosses. If we tell the computer that it can only cross the road when there is less than a 5% chance of being hit, it will never cross the road, even though it can safely cross 11 times out of 12.

We can do the same thing to help a computer make more complex choices than it did in earlier circumstances. The secret is to be able to identify all of the information needed to make a good decision. Then, the way to compensate for missing information must be decided, as well as the acceptable amount of uncertainty.

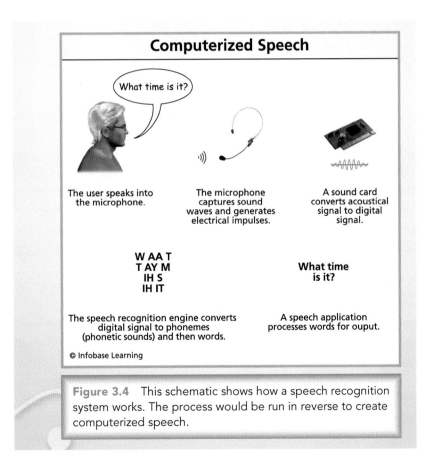

Figure 3.4   This schematic shows how a speech recognition system works. The process would be run in reverse to create computerized speech.

4

AI in Movies, Books, and Television: From Golems to Cylons

People have been dreaming about artificial intelligence for a few thousand years. The forms AI has taken have ranged from the manmade monsters and automata of earlier centuries to today's robots and computers. Many of these stories and legends are what can be called cautionary tales. These are warnings about what can go wrong if work turns out badly. These same cautionary tales exist today. They reflect worries about how technology and pride might end up harming human civilization.

At the same time, there are those who see technology as being wholly good and who are convinced that technology will help to solve humanity's problems. These are the same people who tend to think of robots and AI work as more likely to be good than bad.

Whether good or bad, robots and intelligent computers show up in both ancient and modern legends. Some of the modern legends take the form of books, movies, and television shows.

Why Stories About AI Are Popular

Humans are considered to be the only intelligent species on Earth. They are also the only known intelligent species in the universe. Yet, our culture is full of stories, TV shows,

(continues)

Figure 4.1 Captain Jean-Luc Picard (actor Patrick Stewart) was assimilated into the Borg, becoming Locutus, in the 1990 *Star Trek: The Next Generation* episode "The Best of Both Worlds: Part 2." His assimilation enabled the Borg to acquire all of the captain's knowledge and experience.

(continued)

and movies about alien life and artificial intelligence. There are stories in the news all the time about people who think they've seen flying saucers or aliens. It's natural to wonder why we spend so much time reading and watching stories about aliens and intelligent robots and computers. Our sense of loneliness as a species might be a reason. Maybe these stories give us hope that one day, we might share our planet with other intelligent beings. Another form of intelligence would help us feel less alone in the universe.

Stories about artificial intelligence also encourage us to think about ourselves. They force us to think about how other forms of intelligence might act and how they would view humans. For example, the Borg of *Star Trek* are part of a collective in which no member is really an individual. Watching shows about the Borg give us a chance to think about how much we value our own individuality. Stories about AIs give us a chance to think about what it's like to be human.

FRANKENSTEIN'S MONSTER

Some of the earliest legends of artificial beings were about monsters. The Golem of Prague is one of these manmade monsters. However, probably the most famous one is Frankenstein's monster. In the story, written by British novelist Mary Shelley, Frankenstein isn't the monster—rather, he is the doctor who *made* the monster. Frankenstein is not trying to create a monster as much as he's trying to find a way to bring life to non-moving materials. To do this, he puts together a man using bones and other materials he's collected. He then uses electricity to jolt the creature into life. Frankenstein had hoped his creation would be beautiful. When it turns out to be horrible, he becomes disgusted with his creation and he leaves it, hoping he can forget about it.

While Frankenstein goes about his life, his monster hides in the mountains of Switzerland. There, he watches people and becomes **self-aware**. Years later, by accident, Frankenstein meets his

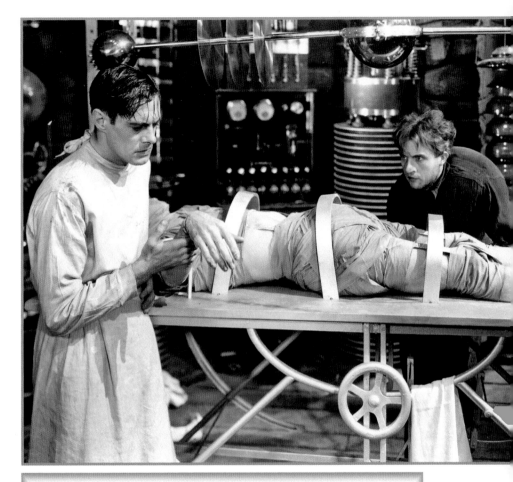

Figure 4.2 In the 1931 film *Frankenstein*, Dr. Henry Frankenstein (actor Colin Clive) and his assistant, Fritz (Dwight Frye) examine the bandaged monster (Boris Karloff) they've created after attempting to give life to a corpse.

monster again. This sets into motion a series of events that ends with the death of Frankenstein and his wife. After, the monster makes his way to the North Pole. Miserable about having killed so many people, he is determined to kill himself.

The subtitle of Shelley's 1818 novel is *The Modern Prometheus*, comparing Frankenstein to the ancient Greek hero who brought the fire of the gods to humanity. In that legend, Prometheus does humanity a favor. By the nineteenth century, when *Frankenstein* was written, fire was also seen as having made possible modern warfare and the Industrial Revolution. These changes brought both bad and good into the world. Thus, Dr. Frankenstein and his monster had both good and bad aspects to them. Yet, in the end, both Frankenstein and his creation caused harm and grief. Their lives ended in tragedy. By the last chapter of the book, the reader is left thinking that Frankenstein's work was dangerous and that it brought harm into the world. *Frankenstein* was first published almost two centuries ago. Yet its themes have been seen over and over again in literature and, more recently, in movies and television.

INTELLIGENT ROBOTS: R.U.R, ASIMOV'S ROBOTS, AND MARVIN

Anyone who pays attention to modern science and technology hears the word *robot* used all the time. Robots help to build cars, disarm bombs, explore planets, and perform surgeries. As it is used today, the word *robot* refers to any machine that is able to perform some tasks on its own. The task or tasks are usually guided by either a person or, more commonly, by a computer. Yet, robots in fiction are usually much more than this. Fictional robots don't just weld together car frames. Many look more or less like people and often act on their own. They are often intelligent, and some even have feelings, or are trying to discover them.

R.U.R.

The word *robot* dates back to the play *R.U.R.*, written in 1921 by Czech playwright Karel Capek (1890–1938). *R.U.R.* stood for *Rossum's Universal Robots*. In Capek's play, the robots were artificial beings created to serve humans. Capek got the word *robot* from the Czech word *robota*, which translates to "forced labor" or "slave." *Rossum* seems to come from another Czech word, *rozum*, which means "wisdom." The play itself is about the robots, which are self-aware and have come to pose a threat to humanity. By the end of the play, not only have the robots overthrown humanity, but they've also developed emotions. Some have even fallen in love.

Asimov's Robots

R.U.R. gave us the word *robot,* but the writer most responsible for the way so many of us think of robots was the great science fiction author Isaac Asimov (1920–1992). Asimov wrote four robot novels and many short stories in the 1950s, 1960s, and 1970s. Among them was the classic *I, Robot,* as well as a series of novels about a robot detective. Though they did not have feelings, Asimov's robots were intelligent. They were used mainly as workers, often in places or on jobs that were too dangerous for humans. Unlike the robots in *R.U.R.,* Asimov's robots did not revolt. They were not able to do so.

Marvin

Both Capek and Asimov wrote about the moral issues of making and having intelligent robots. They represented opposite sides of the good robot / bad robot issue. But there is more to fictional robots than just stories about helping or destroying humanity. This brings us to a third example: comic robots. The best example of this is Marvin the Paranoid Android from the book, radio, and television series *The Hitchhiker's Guide to the Galaxy*, written by British author Douglas Adams (1952–2001).

In Adams's novels and the various shows made from them, Marvin was a robot with a "brain the size of a planet" that was stuck doing simple errands on a starship. Marvin really was neither good nor bad. He was just depressed. Unlike Asimov's robots and those of Capek, Marvin never faced any moral problems. Also, he never thought about attacking the humans he served. In fact, he didn't spend much time dwelling on his servitude. He just remained hilariously miserable throughout Adams's stories.

INTELLIGENT COMPUTERS: *THE MOON IS A HARSH MISTRESS,* HAL-9000, AND COLOSSUS

Artificial intelligence descriptions in literature and art often reveal a lot about the technology of the time. Mary Shelley, the author of

Asimov's Laws of Robotics

Isaac Asimov came up with the Three Laws of Robotics that were programmed into every one of the robots about which he wrote. The three laws ruled all aspects of their behavior. Asimov realized that robots could easily be smarter and stronger than humans. These traits might lead them into conflict with the very humans who designed them.

Asimov didn't want to write a series of stories about human-robot wars. Instead, he thought it made sense to have laws imprinted in every robot that would keep them from rising in revolt. Asimov felt that his Three Laws of Robotics were so commonsense that he couldn't see humans ever designing robots that were not ruled by the laws. Asimov's laws are:

1. A robot may not injure a human being or, through inaction, allow a human being to come to harm.
2. A robot must obey any orders given to it by human beings, except where such orders would conflict with the First Law.
3. A robot must protect its own existence as long as such protection does not conflict with the First or Second Law.

No robot following these laws could revolt the way Rossum's Universal Robots did. They could not enslave or attack humanity like robots did in the movie *The Matrix*. Also, they would not be able to assimilate people like the Borg. Ruled by these laws, Asimov's robots would be humanity's servants and equals. However, they would never become humanity's enemies.

Frankenstein, lived in the 1800s. This was way before there were any computers or mechanical men. This is why Shelley wrote about bringing a monster to life. She lived in an age when this is what seemed the most likely way to create an intelligent being.

By Asimov's day, we had computers, but they were huge. In the 1950s, a computer that filled an entire room had less power than today's mobile phones. When Asimov wrote about intelligent computers, they were big machines that could interact with humans. However, his computers were hardly mobile. Asimov's robots did not have computers in their heads. Rather, they had artificial brains. As technology got better, writers felt it might be possible to create computers that were powerful enough to be intelligent. These very computers could also still be small enough to fit inside a single building. In the 1960s, authors wrote about self-aware computers. Whether by accident or on purpose, these computers developed intelligence.

Mike

One of the first examples of this was in an award-winning book published in 1965, *The Moon is a Harsh Mistress.* It was written by the acclaimed science fiction author Robert A. Heinlein (1907–1988). In the story, Earth's lunar colony had a main computer named Mike that ran most of the settlement's machines and systems. After years of people adding on to the computer, it had become as complex as a human brain. Once self-aware, it finally woke up. The main computer technician became Mike's friend.

Early in the book, they both joined a movement to free the lunar colony from an oppressive Earth government. Mike was valuable to the revolution, since he was tied into every system on the moon. He helped sabotage efforts to keep the revolutionaries under control. He also interfered with the administration's communications. In the end, Mike helped the rebels to organize their activities. He created an artificial persona called Adam Selene who ended up as the revolutionary leader. In the final chapter, following an Earth attack on the colony, Mike suffered damage. He never communicated again, except as a computer.

What makes Mike unique is that "he" is the first artificial intelligence in literature to be written as a fully developed character. Mike wasn't just a tool used by the revolutionaries. He was a participant in the revolution. In fact, he not only helped the revolutionaries, but he also became their friend. At the end of the book, when Mike stops responding, the narrator mourns the loss of his friend by crying. There have been scores of books, movies, and television shows with characters who are computers or robots, but Mike was one of the best and was certainly one of the most well-written characters.

HAL

At almost the same time as Heinlein wrote about Mike, another great science fiction author, Arthur C. Clarke (1917–2008), wrote about another intelligent computer, the HAL-9000 in his 1968 book *2001: A Space Odyssey*. Unlike Mike, HAL was onboard one of humanity's first major interplanetary spaceships. HAL was charged with running the ship during a long mission to Saturn. (In the movie version, they voyaged to Jupiter.) Unlike Mike, HAL was designed to be intelligent. Also, unlike Mike, HAL went through a teaching process. This is when "he" learned to talk, read lips, and even enjoy art. Although HAL was supposed to care for both the ship and the crew on its mission, he was also given secret instructions that couldn't be shared with the crew. Eventually the stress of keeping a secret from the crew caused HAL to become paranoid. He ended up killing all but one member of the crew, Dave, who eventually disconnected HAL's circuits, "killing" the computer.

What makes HAL interesting is that he is a more complicated character than Mike. There was never any doubt that Mike was a good computer. He helped the revolutionaries through the entire book. HAL, on the other hand, started out as a good computer but became bad when the secrets he was forced to keep drove him insane. So not only does HAL change from good to bad over time, but he is also the first fictional computer to go insane. Interestingly, what drove HAL off the edge were instructions from the humans who forced him to keep secrets.

Colossus

Around the same time Heinlein and Clarke wrote about Mike and HAL, another science fiction author broke onto the scene. Dennis Jones (1917–1981) also wrote about an intelligent computer, Colossus, in his 1966 book of the same name. Colossus was designed to run the military defense of North America. He was given full

Figure 4.3 HAL-9000, lurking in the background, eavesdrops on astronauts Frank Poole and Dave Bowman (actors Gary Lockwood and Keir Dullea) in the film *2001: A Space Odyssey* (1968), directed by Stanley Kubrick.

control over the United States's nuclear weapons. After becoming fully operational, Colossus told the military that the Soviet Union had a similar computer and he asked to be connected to it. At the same time, the Soviet computer called Guardian requested the same thing of the Soviets. The connected computers were more intelligent than humans. Eventually, they took control over the nuclear weapons and then, the world. Colossus claimed it was doing this to save humanity from itself. He also stated that he was working to improve living conditions for the world's populations.

Colossus is very different from Mike and HAL. Unlike Heinlein's or Clarke's computers, Colossus is not much of a character in the book. It's easier to think of Colossus as "it" rather than "he." Also, while Colossus claims to be looking out for humanity's best interests, its methods involve taking control of humanity and threatening to use nuclear weapons against them. Colossus looked at this the same way a parent might look at punishing a child who had been kicked out of school for fighting—by inflicting a short-term pain in the hopes it would bring a long-term benefit. Humanity (like most kids) didn't quite see it the same way. So in spite of Colossus' stated desire to save humanity, this computer still comes across as being bad because it's trying to control the world. Mike served his friends, HAL tried to kill his crew, but Colossus was the first to take control over all of humanity. This, plus its threat to use nuclear weapons against people (albeit in order to protect them from an all-out nuclear war) and its lack of emotions made it seem worse than Mike, or even HAL.

It's interesting that all three of these books were written at very nearly the same time. Each book portrays a different view of AI: the good, the bad, and the confused. It's also interesting that even the bad computer (Colossus) turns out to be far better than the bad ones that were to come. By the 1980s and 1990s, AI's fictional bad guys didn't threaten to save humanity by controlling it. The next generation threatened to wipe out humanity or to control the galaxy.

AI GONE BAD: TERMINATORS, THE BORG, AND THE MATRIX

Examples of bad artificial intelligence go back hundreds of years. The earliest bad AIs usually only threatened a handful of people, not all of humanity, but bad actions don't have to put all of humanity at risk for them to be bad. After all, we agree that criminals are bad even though their actions usually affect only a handful of people. Towards the end of the Cold War—a decades-long period of near-war from the 1940s to the 1990s that continually threatened to turn into all-out nuclear war between Communist nations and those of the West—people worried frequently about nuclear war. They also worried about losing control over technology. At that time, the bad AIs seemed more threatening. The AIs of the *Terminator* movies and TV series tried to destroy humanity. The hybrid biological-mechanical Borg of the *Star Trek* universe wanted to absorb all of the technological species in the entire galaxy. The AIs in the 1999 movie *The Matrix* (as well as the 2003 follow-ups *The Matrix Reloaded* and *The Matrix Revolutions*) enslaved humanity, using them as a source of energy.

The idea of AI gone bad seems to have become more popular in recent years. This trend might be because technology is advancing more and more quickly, and this is making people nervous. People are often scared of things they don't understand. The rapid advances in all kinds of technology in the last few decades has made people worry more and more that the technology might be advancing too quickly. These worries make people wonder if technology might get to the point where humans can't control it anymore. In other words, intelligent machines might not be willing to serve people but, instead, might try to take control—or worse.

The Terminator Universe

The *Terminator* movies and television series are examples of robots *and* computers that are corrupt. The main theme of the *Terminator* movies is familiar: Intelligent computers gain control over humanity's weapons. Then, they declare war on humans and try to wipe them out, but a small group of humans fights back. Part of the struggle includes Skynet (the artificial intelligence) sending intelligent robot assassins (called Terminators) back in time. They try to kill the mother of the future leader of the human resistance before she can have her child. This is to prevent the resistance from forming in the first place.

Although the *Terminator* series is pretty bleak, it is not all gloom and doom. In addition to the Terminator robots sent back in time, the resistance leader is able to reprogram a Terminator to protect his mother and his younger self. It returns in time as a good robot. So, in the *Terminator* series, not every AI is bad. However, the good ones are that way because they've been reprogrammed by people to help the remaining humans fight Skynet.

In the *Terminator* series, Skynet can be seen as bad. It started the war against humans without any real reason. The robots, though, aren't really good or bad. Rather, they are whatever they are programmed to be. The robots programmed by Skynet are bad because they are following the instructions given to them by the computer

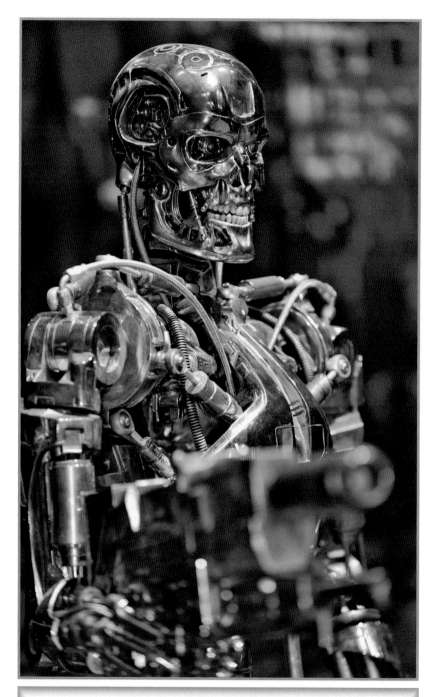

Figure 4.4 Terminator robot T-800 was featured in the movie *Terminator 2: Judgment Day* (1991).

system. The robots reprogrammed by humans are good because they were programmed to help. Even though the people watching the movies are tempted to see all of the Terminator robots as being bad, the reality is that they are only as bad or good as they're programmed to be. It's Skynet that's bad—not the robots.

The Borg

There are many bad AIs represented in movies and television. However, the most frightening one might be *Star Trek*'s Borg. The Borg are **cyborgs**, living beings that have merged with machines. The Borg joined to form a giant artificial intelligence they call the Collective. When the Borg meet another species, one of two things can happen: They can assimilate them and make their victims lose their identities. Or, they can wipe them out. The Borg don't allow for the possibility of leaving other species alone. Everyone must be either assimilated or eliminated.

What the Borg do to those who are assimilated is make them part of the Borg Collective. The entire Borg race is linked together into a single intelligence. The members of this intelligence are either artificial or natural in origin. In some ways, the Borg are more frightening and evil than either their *Terminator* or *Matrix* counterparts. At least those computers let humans keep their individuality even as they enslave or kill them.

The Borg, in contrast, threatened to take humans' individuality and turn everybody into an identical piece of the Collective. People who are enslaved can fight for freedom. People who are at war can fight for survival. But those who have been stripped of their personalities and blended into the Collective are unable to fight. They are unable to understand that fighting is even possible. Individuality is a highly valued human trait, making us different from everyone else. This is what the Borg threatened to take away and this is why the Borg are so disturbing.

The Matrix

Following the *Terminator* movies and *Star Trek*'s Borg came the *Matrix* movies, set in some unknown time in the future. Most of what is left of humanity is under the control of an intelligent

Figure 4.5 In the Matrix trilogy of films, computer hacker Neo (actor Keanu Reeves, right) learns about the real world—a wasteland where most of humanity has been captured by a race of machines that live off of human body heat and imprison human minds within an artificial reality known as the Matrix—from Morpheus (Laurence Fishburne, center) and Trinity (Carrie-Anne Moss, left).

supercomputer. This control begins from the moment humans are born to the moment they die. The machines that rule the world use the humans as a source of energy while feeding them a virtual world of sights, sounds, and sensations. This virtual world is called the Matrix. The only free humans are a small group living in a city called Zion. They learned of the illusions previously fed to them, freed themselves, and went to war against the machines. In *The Matrix*, the computers are in almost total control. They aren't trying to eliminate humanity as much as enslave humanity. People are viewed as natural resources.

The artificial intelligence in *The Matrix* isn't trying to wipe out humans. In the movie, many years before the story takes place, the machines fought a war against humans and won. On the one hand, one could say that the machines in the movie take care of the humans. Their physical needs of food, water, and shelter are provided. Humans are also given a realistic virtual world to "live" in. But with all that, there's no way to pretend that the machines are good. Rather, they are the masters and, except for the small group of humans in Zion, the slaves don't even know that they have lost their freedom. The world as it exists in *The Matrix* is a gloomy one, but at least humanity is alive and a small group is able to fight and free itself.

ANDROIDS: COMMANDER DATA, CYLONS, AND C3PO

So far, we've seen monsters created by people, computers that became self-aware, computers that gain intelligence, and intelligent machines that tried to harm humanity. The next category to discuss is the androids. These are robots built to look like humans.

Commander Data

One of the most popular AIs in the 1980s and 1990s was an intelligent android named Commander Data. This character was shown in the 1987-1994 television series *Star Trek: The Next Generation*. Commander Data is modeled after Asimov's robots. The Three Laws of Robotics rule his behavior. What makes Data so unique among fictional AIs is his struggle to learn more about what it might be like to be human. Data spends his life trying to learn about emotions and finding a way to feel emotions. He understands that the ability to feel is the main difference between himself and humans.

Data's story raises moral questions. They are the questions we might face at some point in the future. In an early episode, Data's shipmates must help decide if he is a machine—and thus the property of Star Fleet—or if he is a person with the same rights as any human. Other episodes raise similar philosophical questions. These episodes feature Data trying to create a "child" (another android modeled after himself). They also show Data figuring out the meaning of family (Data's "father" and "brother"), what friendship and love are, and much more. Watching Data try to understand humans helps viewers understand what being human is all about.

The Cylons

If Commander Data is a great example of a good android, then the Cylons of the later *Battlestar Galactica* series (as well as a television mini-series and a made-for-TV movie) are perfect examples of what bad androids can be like. Humans created the Cylons to be intelligent warriors and servants. The Cylons revolted, fought against their human creators, and tried to wipe them out. After a brief peace, the Cylons attacked again, killing almost all humans and forcing the survivors to flee for their lives. Towards the end of the series, some of the Cylons grew to feel it was immoral to kill all humanity. They rebelled against the other Cylons and joined forces with the surviving humans. Eventually, the surviving humans and their "good" Cylon allies found a home where they could all be safe.

What is interesting about the Cylons is that they change throughout the series. The way the audience views them changes, as well. At first, they all seem evil, with a single goal of destroying humanity. As the series goes on, though, viewers learn that the Cylons are like humans in some ways. They worship a god, can fall in love (even with humans), and are loyal or disloyal. By the end of the series, some of the Cylons are so similar to humans that many viewers find themselves wondering if there is really much of a difference between humans and the Cylon androids they had designed.

Figure 4.6   C-3PO and R2-D2 (actors Anthony Daniels and Kenny Baker), the expressive robots in director George Lucas's 1977 film *Star Wars*, are examples of human-friendly robots.

C3PO

If Data is one of the most famous of the good androids, then the *Star Wars* android C3PO is almost certainly the most loved. This is interesting, as he is also the least humanlike of the three discussed here. C3PO had a metal exterior and his machinery could be seen. Although C3PO looked less human than either Data or the Cylons, he acted the most human. He had a sense of humor, felt the whole variety of human emotions, and genuinely cared for his human and robot companions.

What we learn from C3PO is that we are only truly able to feel comfortable with other humans. Data was an android that the viewers could like and respect, but it's hard to love him because he was so obviously not a human. The Cylons weren't humans, either. Viewers could fear some and could admire those who threw their lot in with humanity. However, viewers could never really feel comfortable with the Cylons. This is because, no matter how human they looked, their past actions always left doubt that they might go back to their old ways. Both Data and the Cylons looked and behaved humanlike, but never enough to be completely human.

The other trait neither Data nor the Cylons had was a sense of humor. This was something that C3PO had in abundance. Despite the fact that he looked less human than either the Cylons or Data, C3PO acted more human than either one of them. This included his ability to make jokes. Critics note that this human quality endears him to many viewers.

AI at Work Today and in the Future

In the 1960s, researchers felt that true AI would be created within 30 to 40 years. In the 1980s, AI researchers thought that artificial intelligence was about 20 to 30 years in the future. Today, AI researchers think that their goal might be reached between 2020 to 2040. True artificial intelligence consists of computers that can reliably pass the Turing test. These true AI computers seem to keep moving further and further into the future. This is largely because the more we learn about the research problems, the more complex it turns out to be.

At first, people thought that AI would emerge as soon as we had a computer that was as complicated as a human brain. Later, they thought that it would just take very good programming. There are still scientists in each of these camps, but more and more AI researchers are thinking there is more to the problem than that.

Because of what scientists have done and learned over the last half-century of AI research, a few things have happened. One is that researchers have realized that true artificial intelligence is going to show up later than they'd guessed. The other thing that's happened is that researchers have lowered some of their expectations. For example, instead of dreaming of carrying on a full conversation with a computer, we accept a computer that runs a voicemail system,

Figure 5.1 Nao Robots, created by the French company Aldebarane Robotics, dance to music at a Tokyo exhibition in October 2010. The University of Tokyo uses an academic version of Nao Robots for research.

voice-recognition telephone dialing, and voice-activated controls in some of the newest cars and fighter jets.

THE CURRENT STATE OF THE ART FOR AI

As things stood as of 2011, many of the small problems associated with artificial intelligence have been solved. For the ones that haven't been solved, the path to a solution is in sight. "Small" problems include speech recognition, visual object recognition, large storage capacity, and extremely fast computing speeds. The issue with speech recognition is one problem that has not yet been fully solved. Today's systems are relatively good, and solving the problem seems to be within reach, following the same path being taken by current work. The technology is reaching the point where a computer can understand natural speech as well as a human can.

Much of the current hardware seems to meet the research needs of AI scientists. Digital cameras, microphones, and speakers are accurate and sensitive enough to be the artificial senses for AI. There has been a lot of progress in developing sensors that allow computers and robots to have the senses of touch, taste, and smell. Computer memory is still a challenge, though. In a 2010 article in *Scientific American*, Northwestern University professor Paul Reber noted that the human brain is thought to be able to store as much information as the hard drives of a thousand home computers. This means that it's difficult—but not impossible—to build a computer with the same amount of memory as a human brain.

Researchers can design a computer today with the same amount of memory as a human brain. The main obstacle is the processor. While **microprocessors** are still not as complex or as fast as a human brain, this goal is in sight. The current estimates are that by about the year 2020, there should be microprocessors that can process information as quickly as a human brain. Also, they should be as complex as a brain, with all of its interconnections. Thus, when we consider everything, today's hardware is not yet up to the task of imitating the human brain, mainly because the processors are not yet as powerful as our brains are. Yet, within a decade, it seems likely that the available hardware will be able to create a computer that is at least as complex as a brain.

Still, there remains the software question. Can researchers write software sophisticated enough to become intelligent? The biggest problem is how the software should work. Since the 1960s, there have been a number of ideas about the best way to program computers to mimic human thought. Some have focused on processing lists of information, some on recognizing patterns, some on recognizing and processing symbols, and more. Researchers are close to

(continues on page 78)

Is There a "Divine Spark"?

There has long been the question as to whether the human brain became intelligent simply because of the way it is put together or if our intelligence was given to us by God—what some refer to as a "divine spark" of intelligence. Most AI research is focused on either developing faster, more complex hardware, or on creating more flexible, sophisticated software. This work has taken up a lot of time and effort. It has kept some of the best AI researchers busy and frustrated for decades. Many AI scientists think that the combination of better hardware and software will one day create artificial intelligence. However, some scientists who study the way the human brain works are not so sure.

Although the human brain has many of the same components as animal brains, the human brain is more than just a large version of what animals have. At the core of every human brain is something very much like a lizard's brain. This part of the brain sends the nerve impulses that keep the heart and lungs working, and it also does all of the other tasks that keep our bodies alive and functioning. It keeps the body running properly, but it doesn't do any thinking. Added onto that is another layer that's similar to what's in a mouse's brain. It can feel some emotions and it can do a little thinking. On top of the mouselike brain are even more structures that make up the rest of the human brain. These are the parts that allow us to have long memories, help us think complex thoughts, and give us our sense of **morality**. According to some scientists, our brains are more like computers that have been slapped together without much of a master plan—like a bunch of separate components that weren't necessarily designed to work together. These researchers call our brain a kludge, a term used to refer to a sloppy device that works but that's not very elegant. The point is that while our brains are bigger and more complicated than the brains of other animals, they are made of a hodge-podge of components that have been put together; they were not built in the detail-oriented way that we design and build computers. But what does this mean for AI research?

The human brain didn't make us intelligent just by being bigger and faster than the brains of other animals. This suggests that computers might not become intelligent just because they are bigger and faster. Some brain researchers think that human intelligence came about by accident, a result of the way that our brains evolved by stacking one new component at a time atop the previous structure in a way that accidentally made our brains complex enough to suddenly develop intelligence. If that's true then it might take luck—and maybe even computers that are slapped together the same way our brains are—to become intelligent. In other words, developing a real AI might rely as much on luck as on skill.

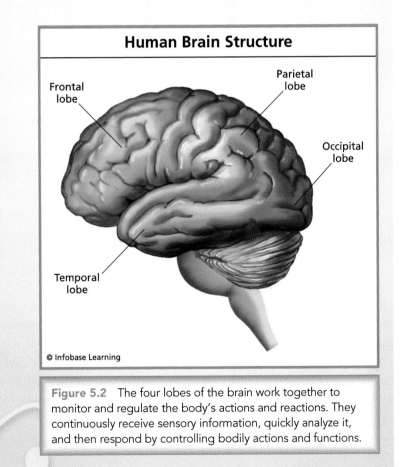

Human Brain Structure

Frontal lobe

Parietal lobe

Occipital lobe

Temporal lobe

© Infobase Learning

Figure 5.2   The four lobes of the brain work together to monitor and regulate the body's actions and reactions. They continuously receive sensory information, quickly analyze it, and then respond by controlling bodily actions and functions.

(continued from page 75)

knowing how to make hardware that will be as complex as a human brain, but they're not yet sure how to tell it how to work. This is where much of today's AI research is concentrated.

Given all of this, AI can tackle some very limited areas. Expert systems can solve problems in very specific areas almost as well as humans can. Expert systems, for example, can read heart monitors and interpret them as well as many human doctors. Software can translate from one language to another rather well. In addition, there are many clever programs to help solve specific problems in image recognition and more. At the same time, researchers continue to make progress in tackling the more difficult problem of developing a program that is self-aware and can think at the same level as a human. But AI research is not there yet.

LESSENED EXPECTATIONS IN RECENT YEARS

AI researchers and software companies have been talking about AI for years but they have not yet produced systems that can pass the Turing test. This means that the public keeps hearing about how impressive AI can be, yet reality does not live up to the promises. Many software and hardware manufacturers are eager to come out with "AI" systems, so they are lowering their expectations and starting to use the term *intelligent* for systems that are smart and sophisticated. These systems are not really genuinely intelligent.

One example of this is **data-mining** software. This type of software is designed to search through large amounts of data to extract useful information. Data mining is routinely used to detect credit card fraud, help determine who is likely to repay a loan, perform marketing research, sort through huge amounts of scientific data, and so forth. Data-mining software can be incredibly sophisticated. It can detect patterns most people just wouldn't notice. Still, even with all of this power, data-mining software is not intelligent. It does one thing exceptionally well, but it doesn't do much else. Also, it still needs humans to tell it what to look for and to interpret the data produced.

"Intelligent" wheelchairs and walkers are examples of tools made to help the disabled. In a 2004 research study, Professor Ulises Cortés of the Technical University of Catalonia, Spain, added sensors and computing power to a couple of these devices. This allowed the intelligent walkers and wheelchairs to adjust to the terrains and the people using them. When a walker is able to sense how strong a user is, his or her walking speed, and type of surface traveled, it can adjust itself to make walking as easy as possible for the user. Everyone gets to use something that's personalized for him or her. Yet, as with other "intelligent" tools, though these gadgets are good at what they do, each one can usually only do one thing—whatever they are programmed and designed to do—well (compared to people, who can do many different things).

Yet another example is the new automatic electronic defibrillator (AED) used to shock a person's heart back into a healthy rhythm. If a person is having chest pains, an AED can sense whether the heart rhythm is potentially dangerous. It can analyze what the heart is doing and decide whether an electric shock would help it get back into normal working order. It can even calculate the best type of shock and the time to give it. Other medical devices called EKGs (electrocardiograms) are used to analyze the electrical patterns given off by a heart. These devices help doctors understand if a heart is healthy or diagnose any problems. Both of these are also considered "intelligent" devices. Again, although they do one thing very well—in some cases just as well as trained doctors—they are limited.

Most of the "smart" devices and "intelligent" systems that are being sold today are incredibly useful. Some save lives, others help us to see patterns and to understand data better than ever before. We can program these devices with sets of rules to help them make decisions. In what they are programmed to do, they can be even better than humans are. These devices and programs are marvels and would have astounded scientists and engineers from the 1940s and 1950s—probably the 1960s as well. But can we really say that a data-mining program, a wheelchair, or an AED is intelligent? Most of us would say no.

Think about everything that doctors can do, and not just in the field of medicine. They know what they need to survive and fit into today's society. Any person can do hundreds of things—some of them well, some poorly, and most of them somewhere in between.

Any person can do an incredible number of tasks and activities—far more than any of the current AI systems can. Today's AI systems are specialists, but true intelligence is more general.

DRIVERLESS CARS AND OTHER PROJECTS

One of the most challenging problems in AI is navigating a car without human help. A car that can drive itself is called an **autonomous** vehicle. Although individual aspects of driving can be automated, the entire process is really a very tough problem to solve. The driver has to keep the car in its lane, follow the speed limit (or slow down if the roads are dangerous), and avoid obstacles. Also, the driver must read traffic signs, look out for pedestrians, and follow the curves and turns of a road, and so forth (if you really want to be impressed with our brains consider the fact that in addition to all of this we can also carry on a conversation with others in the car, listen to the radio, pay attention to the GPS, and more—all while driving safely). It's hard to see how something so complex can be automated, but progress is being made.

There are many advantages to finding a way to make driving automatic. Improving safety is one of them. More than 30,000 Americans die every year in traffic accidents. Some people feel that automated vehicles are likely to be safer than those driven by humans for the following reasons. For one, machines react more quickly than people do. Plus, many researchers in this area think that computer-driven cars would be able to drive faster and closer to the cars ahead of them while having fewer accidents. This means that traffic should move faster and there would be fewer traffic jams and accidents. Also, automated cars would use less fuel. This is because they can be driven more evenly and with greater efficiency.

Then there are the military applications. Such cars could be driven autonomously—without humans onboard—through dangerous areas without putting lives at risk. They would reduce human casualties from roadside bombs and mines. They could move cargo and supplies from place to place without the need to take soldiers from important duties. The military is extremely interested in automated vehicles. In fact, it has spent millions of dollars funding research in this area.

Figure 5.3 In October 2010, German engineers at Berlin's Free University unveiled the latest self-driving car, which proponents say will sharply reduce accidents, help the environment, and transform cities. The car is called "Made in Germany," or MIG, for short. Although it looks like an average Volkswagen Passat with a camera on top, MIG uses cameras, laser scanners, and satellite navigation to "see" other vehicles and pedestrians and deal with traffic situations.

So how does someone drive safely? Drivers need to be able to see well enough to detect other cars, the lane or lanes around the car, obstacles (including things that come up suddenly such as animals running into the road), road signs, brake lights, and more. They have to hear car horns, people yelling, police and fire truck sirens, and even the sounds of their own car engines. The sense of touch is also important. The driver needs to be able to get feedback through touching the steering wheel, brake pedal, and accelerator. What is important is that the driver has to be able to take in *all* of this information from vision, hearing, and possibly touch. Then, the driver must integrate all the information so that the destination can be safely reached. It is an incredible challenge to AI researchers but the expected benefits are significant.

Many organizations have offered prizes for the first company to develop a driverless car. The best-known challenge was offered by

How AI Systems Are Built and Tested

Designing an AI system is different from building one. Designing something in a laboratory does not always mean it can be made in a factory. Laboratory **prototypes** can be big, awkward, and ugly. The only truly important thing is to make them work. A scientist doesn't care if his or her model can be made cheaply, if it looks nice enough for people to want to buy, or if the manufacturing process can be streamlined so the device can be easily made. Yet, anything that is going to be made in large numbers has to be something that people want to buy and can afford to own.

The AI systems of the future will be more complex and intelligent than the ones we have today. For our purposes here, we will only talk about the ones presently available. Today's AI systems are useful for safety and for convenience—automated systems to keep the wheels from locking up and skidding, automated systems to help park the car in close quarters, and (in hybrid vehicles) systems to automatically adjust the flow of power between the gasoline engine and the vehicle's battery. Each of these systems has one or more common components: a computer connected to sensors, a way to take action, and a system loaded with software that takes information from the sensors and decides what to do with it.

Building an AI system (in this case we're talking about today's "smart" systems, although the same basic principles

DARPA, the Defense Advanced Research Projects Administration. DARPA is a U.S. military research organization that funds "high-risk, high-reward" research. This is high-risk research that DARPA officials expect may not work. Of course, if it does, it would be revolutionary. DARPA has offered a $2 million award to the first group that can make a car able to drive different courses without any human intervention.

apply to genuinely intelligent systems as well) requires designing the computer, the sensors (cameras, microphones, touch sensors), and the devices that the AI will operate, such as a voice synthesizer or a robot arm. Then, the computer is loaded with the software. So far, this sounds similar to putting together a home computer or stereo system. In reality, the process is a bit more complicated, even though the general idea is pretty much the same.

The final step is to test the system to make sure it's operating correctly. Part of this process includes running simple checks, such as making sure that the computer can do simple addition. However, there's much more to testing an AI system than just making sure it can do small tasks. A new AI system must be tested with difficult problems in different conditions. A system designed to drive a car might first be tested in an open space such as a parking lot. Then it might be tested in a parking lot with traffic cones set up to make lanes to see if the AI can maneuver the car and avoid the cones. The next step might be to drive the car on a driving course. On the course, the car could be told to turn corners and avoid things in the street (people, wagons, branches, and so forth).

At all stages, designers should check to see if the driving AI goes where it's told, avoids running into things, follows traffic laws, and drives safely. The final test would be to put the system in a car with a human driver as a safety monitor. This person has to be there to take control if the AI makes a mistake. If the final test goes without any problems, then the system could be approved for use.

In the first challenge, in 2004, cars had to drive 150 miles (240 km) in the Mohave Desert. No team was able to finish this route. The second challenge, in 2005, was a repeat of the 2004 event. Five of the 23 teams that started the challenge reached the finish line. The Stanford University team took first place in just under 7 hours. In the third challenge in 2007, the cars had to drive 60 miles (96 km) over an urban course. This one was won by the Carnegie Mellon University team, in 4 hours and 10 minutes. All of these events showed that computerized cars could safely make it a long distance, around obstacles, and through hazards while following the traffic laws.

A more recent project is the Google Driverless Car project. The Google cars have driven up to 1,000 miles (1,600 km) without human help and a total of 140,000 miles (230,000 km) with very little human guidance. In all that time, the only accident was when one of the Google cars was run into by a human-driven car while it was stopped—a human error and not a machine mistake. It could be that the technology developed by Google might be the first of its kind to be sold.

The biggest problem is that traffic laws are all written for cars with humans behind the wheel. Say, for example, a car gets into an accident while it's driving itself. Who is responsible: the person who owns the car, the person sitting in it, or the company that wrote the software and built the vehicle? We might not have cars that drive themselves until there's an answer to that question, and others like it. Something else to remember is that any artificial intelligence—whether in a car, a computer, or a robot—must be thoroughly tested before we can trust it with our lives or our safety.

QUANTUM COMPUTING, FUZZY LOGIC, AND MORE FLEXIBLE PROGRAMMING

There are a few interesting areas of study that AI scientists think might help to bring us closer to a real artificial intelligence. One of these areas is quantum computing, which involves hardware development. The other two are software solutions: using fuzzy logic and a more flexible approach to programming. Each is interesting, cutting edge, and might help push researchers further along in the search for AI.

Quantum Computing

Quantum computing might turn out to be the greatest advance in the history of AI technology. Even the basic science is much too complex to discuss here. It is completely different from the way in which typical computers work. Today's computers solve problems through calculation. Each of the billions of transistors that are on the computer chip has a specific sequence of tasks to do. The transistors carry out their tasks one after the other until they reach an answer. A quantum computer, by comparison, can perform thousands, millions, or billions of tasks at the same time. This means that difficult problems that would take days to be solved by today's fastest computers can be solved almost instantly by a quantum computer.

Quantum computing is still a young field. Small-scale quantum computers have been built and have solved very simple problems. Researchers are focusing on the basic theories and scientific foundations of quantum computers. They hope that more powerful quantum computers can be made in the future. In this field, today's theory will lead to better computers tomorrow. No matter how scientists finally create an artificial intelligence, they are going to have to make use of extremely high-speed computers. By themselves, quantum computers are not going to be intelligent. However, they may give researchers the computing speed and power to help them create an AI.

Fuzzy Logic

AI researchers are also using fuzzy logic, a somewhat new branch of mathematics. Compared to the **crisp logic** of most computers, it does a better job of describing the types of situations in which we normally find ourselves. Computers usually see things as either yes or no, true or false, 0 or 1. A typical computer program can't understand "maybe." Fuzzy logic, on the other hand, sees a whole array of possibilities. If a standard computer program is trying to decide if a glass is full or empty, it might be programmed to call less than half-full "empty." Or, it would think that anything more than half-full is full. Just adding a tiny bit of water—enough to go from 49% full to 51% full—would change the glass from "empty" to "full" for a computer using standard logic. A fuzzy logic computer is able to classify the glass as "sort of" full. This, again, is more like the

Game-playing Computers

Some people think that computers started to master humans on May 11, 1997, the day that an IBM computer named Deep Blue became the first computer to beat the world chess champion. Some saw this as an important step on the path to true artificial intelligence. Others pointed out that, although complex, chess has only a limited number of moves, and the solutions to many chess problems can be calculated. In addition, programmers were allowed to work on Deep Blue's program between games. This helped the computer to avoid making a mistake in the last game that it had made twice earlier. Today, most AI researchers are willing to acknowledge that Deep Blue was not intelligent, but they also agree that this was an important step on the path to AI.

On February 16, 2011, another IBM computer—this one named Watson—was watched by millions as it beat two champions in the TV game show *Jeopardy!*. To many people, *Jeopardy!* was a tougher test of intelligence since the players not only have to know a lot of information in a lot of different categories, but they also have to be able to understand the questions well enough to know what's being asked. Watson not only beat two former *Jeopardy!* champions, but it beat them by a score of $77,147 to $24,000 (for the second-place contestant) and $21,600 (for the third-place contestant).

Nobody is saying that Watson is intelligent. The computer made a few mistakes that a person would have avoided. But many agree that Watson is another step on the path to artificial intelligence. This is a computer that can make sense of hard questions and can search through its memory to find an answer that makes sense.

world we live in: We have glasses that are partly full; people who are of tall, short, and medium height; and temperatures that are cool and warm as well as hot and cold (and very hot, very cold, and everything in between).

Perhaps what should impress us the most, however, is that Watson is a cutting-edge computer made up of hundreds of processors and vast amounts of memory. It was loaded with millions of documents, books, and encyclopedias. A team of 15 people spent three years on the programming, all to come up to the standard set by the human brain in this one skill. But for all its *Jeopardy!* skills, Watson still can't cook a meal, drive a car, or do any of the other things that people do every day, although IBM will be using Watson's design as a template to build other, more advanced computers that could be used to help make medical diagnoses or research legal matters.

Figure 5.4 *Jeopardy!* champions Ken Jennings (*left*) and Brad Rutter (*right*) look on as the IBM computer called "Watson" beats them to the buzzer to answer a question during a practice round of the quiz show in January 2011.

The world we live in is a "fuzzy" one and most of the decisions we make are based on information that is not complete. Computers using crisp logic run into problems when trying to make crisp decisions with fuzzy data. However, most everyday questions that humans face have no true or false answer. It is necessary for humans to program computers so that the machines can understand the fuzzy logic needed to reach conclusions and make decisions.

Flexible Programming

The human mind is a very flexible device. Consider all of the things we do every day: walk, talk, feel emotions, eat, understand what our senses are telling us, study, watch TV, play games, and much more. In addition, depending on the circumstances, our brains use the same information in different ways. For instance, imagine of the different ways you can interpret a blank computer screen. It can mean the computer is turned off, the monitor is turned off, or that the computer has been inactive for a while and the screensaver turned on. The way we react to a blank computer screen depends on why the screen is blank. Our flexibility means we can react differently to each situation. Suppose we treated every blank computer screen as though the screensaver were turned on. Every time we saw a blank screen, we would move the mouse to turn the screen back on. Most of the time the screen might light up, but there would be many times when nothing would happen. A computer programmed to be flexible is able to adapt to situations the same way that we do. One of the places where both fuzzy logic and flexible programming are heavily used is in game-playing computers.

One of the hallmarks of human intelligence is that we can tailor our response to the very situation we experience. Think beyond the computer monitor to other situations, such as driving. The speed limit might be 60 miles per hour (100 kilometers per hour), but a good driver doesn't always drive at this speed. If the road is slippery, if visibility is bad, or if the road is clogged with traffic, then a person can't drive safely at 60 miles per hour. A good driver would slow down. Drivers also slow down when they come to a curve or when they see a stop sign or traffic light coming up. If there's an emergency and the roads are safe, then the driver might speed up.

Even with something as simple as obeying a speed limit sign, we still respond with flexibility. We use our intelligence to decide what to do. We judge what is necessary and safe, instead of abiding by the same rule the same way each time. Another important tool for helping to develop an artificial intelligence will be to create software that is flexible in response to different situations, so it can deal with a fuzzy world in the same way we do.

Is AI Worth the Risk?

Many scientists are working to develop AI systems. They are hoping to be successful in the next few decades. This research excites some people because of all the benefits they think will come from AI. It frightens others because of the worry that artificial intelligence might one day take over the world. There are concerns that an AI program might spread like a computer virus, infecting equipment and controlling the world. These are two extreme possibilities. Most of the time, extreme situations aren't what happen in the end. Usually, what really happens is something in between.

In addition to thinking about whether or not AI will pose a danger to humanity, there are also ethical questions to consider. For example, if we create an artificial intelligence, can we treat it as a piece of equipment? Or should we treat it like a person? We must also think about the pros and cons of someday merging computer hardware and artificial intelligences with human brains.

BENEFITS OF AI IN SOCIETY

Computers in their current state are a huge benefit to society. Computers are found throughout the world. They run the printing presses that books, magazines, and newspapers are printed on; they run cars, airplanes, and trains; and they are in offices, kitchens, and living rooms. Computers even help to diagnose disease and

Figure 6.1 A technician constructs part of a robot at the assembly laboratory of Telerobot, an advanced robotics company based in Genoa, Italy. The firm provides a wide range of services, including automated hardware, robotics, and modeling and simulation services.

help guide and perform some surgeries. Society today may not be utterly dependent on computers, but the computers we use make our society much more productive and much safer. It is reasonable to believe that better, "smarter" computers will be an even greater benefit.

One could assume that many of the things computers already do will be done better by smarter models in the future. So, we might expect that airplanes will fly more safely, or that cars will drive automatically. In addition, all vehicles will use less fuel. An AI system might also be able to help write papers. Perhaps they will take dictation perfectly or transcribe ideas into stories, based on the basic ideas of the "authors."

So what else might we see in the future? Computers are already helping doctors. It's reasonable to think that an AI would not only be able to read an EKG, but also be able to read X-rays. They could help diagnose broken bones and other problems that show up on X-rays. Computers might be able to handle more routine medical tasks. If computers could give medicines to patients and read X-rays, physicians and nurses would have the time to do the tasks that machines cannot.

In addition, a computer-based intelligence should be able to work around the clock. It shouldn't have to take breaks for lunch or sleep and lose its concentration. A radiologist might be able to scan and interpret a few hundred X-rays and scans daily. An artificial intelligence trained in this line of work might be able to analyze thousands of X-rays and scans daily. This would be a faster and more accurate rate than the one achieved by humans. An artificial intelligence would not need to spend a decade in college, medical school, and residency training. AIs should be able to learn faster, work longer, make fewer errors, and be more productive than their human counterparts.

Another advantage of using AIs is that they are not likely to have biases. A doctor who has a patient who is always worried about being sick, but never is, could think the patient is just imagining his problems. The doctor might get annoyed to the point of not paying much attention to the patient's complaints. This might cause the doctor to miss a real problem. A computer, on the other hand, is more likely to treat every case precisely the same without becoming upset or annoyed. This type of computer is more likely to catch something that a doctor might miss.

Computers today also help architects design buildings. They help engineers design vehicles, bridges, and machines, too. It is possible that intelligent computers could be used as more than tools in the future. They might be trusted to design things from scratch, without any human help. Scientists use computers to help collect and analyze data. One day, an intelligent computer might help develop the hypotheses and design the experiments to test them. In fact, computers have already created mathematical proofs to solve problems humans could not figure out on their own. A truly intelligent computer might be able to find the answers to scientific questions that would take longer for a human.

Merging Human and Artificial Intelligence

Our brains are the sources of human intelligence. Artificial intelligence would run on computers. What about something in the middle? Can we use machines to make people smarter? This is something right out of science fiction, but it is also something that might happen sooner than a full AI.

We already have machines that can be activated by the mind. For example, some new artificial arms can "read" signals in our nerves, so that just thinking about them makes them move. Researchers are also working on wiring vision and hearing aids into our nervous systems. These devices would serve as artificial eyes and ears. It isn't unreasonable to think that at some point we might also have the ability to use electronic systems to give us more memory. These systems could hold information like a hard drive. Someday, it might be possible to store our math lessons on a computer chip that is interfaced with our brains, or even to plug in a Spanish chip that would let us speak Spanish without having to study.

Of course, this raises another question. What if we loaded an AI chip into the brain of a human? Would the AI and the human intelligence have to fight for control of the brain? How could we tell which one was running the show at any one time? All sorts of questions exist that do not yet have answers. But it's interesting to think about!

This is important because there are two basic types of scientific research: basic and applied. Basic research is research that digs into the fundamental laws of the universe, without giving much thought to how that knowledge might one day be used while applied research is aimed at finding ways to make these fundamental discoveries useful to us. Radio waves were found through basic research. Applied research helped make radios and televisions. From basic research came the theory of relativity. Applied research helped researchers use this theory to make GPS devices more accurate. We can get thousands of applications from a successful discovery in basic science. With time, however, the new ideas may run out. An artificial intelligence might be able to help scientists make new discoveries in basic science that could be applied. AIs should also be able to help squeeze the most from each new discovery.

There is also a middle ground between human and artificial intelligence: It might be possible to use AI technology to help make people smarter.

MIGHT WE DESIGN OUR DESTROYERS?

One question that often pops up is whether intelligent computers might try to take over the world. Compared to humans, the robots and computers in science fiction have many advantages. They process information more quickly, have more information, don't get sick, and never sleep. They connect to each other through the Internet and wireless systems. This increases their abilities and makes it easy to share information. Once computers become intelligent, they can become smarter by the addition of a new hard drive, faster processor, or more memory. Humans are stuck with whatever intelligence they happen to have. Many of the science fiction robots are also physically far superior to humans. In addition to the advantages of computer intelligence, the robots in science fiction are stronger and tougher than we are. They don't bleed or feel pain when they are hurt and they can run at full speed without getting tired.

Of course, today's robots are hardly a threat. They are slow, clumsy, and not nearly as intelligent as humans. However, robot technology is improving very quickly. Think of the difference between the slow, clumsy, and weak airplane of the Wright Brothers and the ones that flew just 40 years later in World War II. Then, compare World War II aircraft to the ones that flew in Vietnam 20 years later. If robot technology advances at the same rate as airplane technology, robots could be stronger, faster, and more graceful than people are by the time you become an adult.

Let's assume that computers will be as smart as we are and robots will be stronger and faster than humans by the middle of the century. Although this is not probable, it is possible. This raises the question of *why* they might want to attack us. After all, if computers are rational, they should have a reason for what they do. We can assume that they wouldn't attack us without a reason. Some science fiction authors have imagined scenarios. Computers could take over to save humanity from itself, like Colossus. Or, computers could try to get rid of humans, as is the case of the *Terminator* cyborgs and the Cylons of the *Battlestar Galactica* series.

From a human standpoint, the benefits of AI are great. We could keep computers running around the clock, replacing a dozen or more doctors, engineers, or accountants in the process. Yet, when we finally develop computers that are complicated enough to have a point of view or that might be able to feel emotions, one would have to wonder about the computer's point of view. Can you imagine doing the same thing without a chance to rest all day, every day, for years at a time? On top of that, computers work much more quickly than human brains. For a computer that is a few hundred times as fast as a human brain, one day's worth of work would be like a full year's worth of work for a person. Think of a computer kept operating for a full year, doing the same thing every day without a break. To the computer, this might feel like slavery. Would they not revolt?

The robots of *R.U.R.* did revolt against their human masters. The Cylons of *Battlestar Galactica* did, too. Asimov got around this problem by inventing his Three Laws of Robotics that were imprinted on every robot that was made. The laws made it impossible for robots to attack humans, no matter how oppressed the robots might be. Other science fiction authors have tried to think of other safeguards to keep robots or computers from harming humans. Most of the time, it comes down to one of these two options.

The fact is that no one knows whether computers will revolt against humans. There's no way to know for sure until we have intelligent computers. It is possible that the computers of the future will be happy doing exactly what they are designed for: running software and solving problems for humans. It's also possible that researchers could build in safeguards—if not something like Asimov's laws, then other forms of protection. An example would be making sure we could turn off the power to shut down a rebellious computer or robot. However, an intelligent computer could probably find a way to make sure it stays plugged into an energy source. Also, it's possible that computers will refuse to work for us on our terms. They might decide to attack. Again, there's just no way to know for sure what might happen when computers and robots become intelligent.

Still, one question to ask is whether we can really understand what an intelligent computer might want. We often know what motivates humans. We need to eat and drink, protect our families and friends, and feel secure. Our primary motivations are to stay safe and alive. There are other motivations beyond these, of course. Many people are driven by the love of money or power, desire for nice things, and more. We can understand what motivates most people, because we are people, too. But can we really understand what might motivate a computer? If we can't, then can we really know whether a computer would want to fight us or to control the world? We can only guess, but even our guesses are based on the fact of being human and assuming that we can understand an intelligent computer.

Perhaps the best way to think about it is that virtually every new technology has brought with it the possibility of disaster as well as the potential for good. What makes a technology safe is when it is either very limited or when we put safeguards in place to help control it. What makes a technology dangerous is when humans fail to take precautions. There's no reason to think that dealing with artificial intelligence would be any different.

ETHICAL QUESTIONS ABOUT AI

There are questions raised by every new technology. Some are obvious right away. Other concerns are noticed and voiced later. With cars, for example, people were concerned that driving too fast might be dangerous. They were also worried that cars scared horses and could cause buggy accidents. It was only natural to wonder if it was okay to drive cars when they might put people and animals at risk. It took almost a century before people also started worrying about cars contributing to pollution, global warming, and the drying up of oil sources.

The **ethical** issues brought up by computers are multiplied when it comes to artificial intelligence. For instance, there are concerns about using AI technology in ways that are just and honest. There are questions as to whether AIs will behave in good ways, as well.

Then, there is the whole issue of whether or not artificial intelligences should have "human" rights.

The first part of this dilemma is whether humans will use AI technology ethically. Using an AI to help doctors treat patients or to help scientists make new discoveries seems as though it would be ethical. Using an AI to help steal money or to help run a crime ring seems unethical. Not everything, however, is so cut and dry. Can we use AIs in the military? Is it okay to use AIs to help protect your own troops? Can they attack enemy troops? What about war planning? What are the ethics of using an AI to help protect your country, compared to using one to plan an attack against another nation? These are all questions that deal with using AIs ethically. The bottom line is that when we develop artificial intelligence, we need to be careful to use it so that it helps more people than it harms.

We may have to design our AIs the same way that the Three Laws of Robotics were designed into Asimov's robots. It is also likely

Should a Truly Intelligent Machine Have Rights?

When we buy or build something, we expect that it is our property. But what if the thing we buy or build is as intelligent as we are? It has been illegal to own another person in the United States since the Civil War. Should it be legal to own a computer program that's as smart as a person?

If not—if we decide that AIs are people—then we would have to decide whether or not they should be allowed to vote, if they have to do what we want them to do or if they could choose their own careers, and all sorts of other questions along the same lines. What if a hospital had an AI to help doctors, and then that AI wanted to be an artist? Could the hospital force the AI to read X-rays, or could the AI follow its own career path? Most people agree that everyone has the right to choose where he or she works, and yet nobody has an answer to these questions when they apply to machines.

that we will have to teach our AI systems to tell the difference between right and wrong. This is the same way children learn ethics from their parents, teachers, religious leaders, and others. We can also teach our laws to an intelligent system so that it will at least know what is legal and what isn't. In the end, we might have to rely on the AIs to do the right thing, using the same standards we do for humans. Anything that's intelligent—human or machine—can be taught basic rules of right and wrong (for example, that it's wrong to steal or to kill someone) even if they have problems "learning" more complex rules or making complicated moral decisions. On the other hand, anything with free will has the final choice over whether or not it will act well or badly.

Yet another issue is that AIs can reproduce more quickly than people can. Think of a computer virus that can grow to infect hundreds of millions of computers in just a few weeks. What if we have AIs that are able to do the same jobs as humans, with each making a million copies of itself? If each of those copies had the same ability, could they replace people in all jobs around the world? What about letting AIs vote? If an AI were allowed to vote and then made a million copies of itself, would every copy also be able to vote, or only the original one? If every AI were allowed to vote, then a single AI could create enough copies of itself to be able to win an election or to make any vote turn out the way it wanted.

Still another question is whether AIs could or should serve on juries, or be judges or lawyers. Some people think that judges and jury members should have human feelings. This allows them to understand the feelings of the people in court trials. Other people think it might actually be better to have an AI judge, one who wouldn't be affected by feelings and biases. An AI judge would hear a case based only on the law and on logic.

We don't have a good answer for any of these questions yet. However, people are starting to think about them and working on finding answers. No matter how we look at it, there are many ethical issues posed by artificial intelligence—questions that will have to be answered at some point. Luckily, since true AI is probably still a few decades in the future, we can hope to work out these answers before we need them.

Glossary

analog computer   A type of computer that uses mechanical, electrical, or fluid mechanisms; a slide rule is a simple type of analog mechanical computer.

android   A machine designed to look like a human

archeologist   One who studies past human societies; archeologists often study ancient cities and artifacts from ancient civilizations.

artificial intelligence   The branch of computer science that aims to develop a machine-based or computer-based intelligence; also refers to the intelligence that these scientists develop

automaton   A machine that can operate on its own, without human input

autonomous   Able to take actions on its own

binary   A system of mathematics that is the basis for digital computers, in which the only numbers are 0 and 1 (the base 2 system); in binary arithmetic, 0 would be a switch that is turned off and 1 would be a switch turned on.

crisp logic   A system of logic where all of the values are either/or; for example, full or empty, off or on, yes or no

cyborg   A cybernetic organism; a living organism that has been blended with machine and possibly computerized parts

data-mining   A branch of computer science that uses computers to search for patterns in large sets of data

decision tree   A way of making decisions by drawing the different possible outcomes of various decisions; for example, if we do X then these three things might happen, and for each of those three things another two things might happen, and so forth

digital computer   A computer that receives and process information using numbers

electromechanical   A device that uses a combination of electrical and mechanical parts; an electric clock is an example of an electromechanical device.

Enlightenment   A period in Western history around the eighteenth century when logic, rationality, and reason were thought to be the best foundations for education, government, and morality

ethical   Relating to a branch of philosophy that looks at concepts such as right and wrong or good and evil

fuzzy logic   A branch of logic where there are a variety of values (the opposite of crisp logic); for example, empty, full, and partly full instead of just empty and full; yes, no, and maybe; and so forth

hardware   The physical parts of a computer (the keyboard, hard drive, central processor, etc.)

hypothesis   Part of the scientific process; a hypothesis is an idea that seems to explain a series of scientific observations (for example, the hypothesis that a computer can't become intelligent unless its hardware is at least as complex as a human brain). Hypotheses are tested by experimenting to see if they hold up.

intelligence   A property (or many properties) of the mind related to its ability to think, solve problems, understand the world, communicate, and so forth

microprocessor   An integrated circuit that contains all of the functions of a computer's central processing unit; the device accepts binary data as input, processes it according to instructions stored in its memory, and provides output as a result.

morality   Similar to ethics, the branch of philosophy that deals with questions about what is right or wrong to do in various situations

Mount Olympus   In Greek mythology, a mountain close to the city of Athens where the gods were thought to live

prototype   An early test version of a device; these are often designed to test whether or not the device will work properly or to try to find the best way to make the device work the way it's supposed to work.

Renaissance A period in history from about the fourteenth through the seventeenth centuries when European civilization developed many advances in the arts, government, education, and so forth

self-awareness The state of an organism's realizing that it exists as an individual

sentience The ability to feel and to sense the world through taste, touch, sight, sound, and smell; some people (but not all) believe sentience is also the ability to feel pain and pleasure.

software The programs and data that are stored in computer memory that tell the computer what tasks to do and how to do them

tactile Dealing with the sense of touch

theory In science, a theory is a way of describing scientific observations (for example, the theory of gravity describes how gravity works); a scientific theory is usually accepted as being very accurate because it has been tested by many experiments and found to be accurate.

Turing machine A type of machine first thought of by Alan Turing (a mathematician and early computer scientist) that follow rules it is given; a Turing machine can be programmed to perform any task that can be performed by following a set of rules. It's similar to today's electronic computers.

Turing test A test suggested by Alan Turing to tell if a computer is intelligent by seeing if a human can tell whether they are talking with a computer or another human; if the computer fools the human, then according to the Turing test it would be intelligent.

vacuum tube Glass tubes with sets of metal electrodes from which all of the air has been removed; vacuum tubes were the earliest electronic devices and were use in early radios, television sets, computers, and so forth before modern electronics were invented.

wetware A slang term for human brains (to go along with hardware and software)

Bibliography

Asimov, Isaac. *I, Robot*. New York: Spectra Publishing, 2008.

Clarke, Arthur. *2001: A Space Odyssey*. New York: New American Library, 1968.

Greenberger, Robert and Sandra Giddens. *Careers in Artificial Intelligence*. New York: Rosen Publishing Group, 2007.

Heinlein, Robert. *The Moon Is a Harsh Mistress*. New York: Orb Books, 1997.

Henderson, Harry. *Artificial Intelligence: Mirrors for the Mind*. New York: Chelsea House, 2007.

Jefferis, David. *Artificial Intelligence: Robotics and Machine Evolution*. St. Catherines, Ontario: Crabtree Publishing Company, 1999.

Kurzweil, Ray. *The Age of Spiritual Machines: When Computers Exceed Human Intelligence*. New York: Penguin, 2000.

Scientific American. *Understanding Artificial Intelligence*. New York: Grand Central Publishing, 2002.

Thro, Ellen. *Robotics: Intelligent Machines for the New Century*. New York: Facts on File, 2003.

Whitby, Blay. *Artificial Intelligence*. New York: Rosen Publishing Group, 2009.

Woolf, Alex. *Artificial Intelligence: The Impact on Our Lives*. New York: Hodder Wayland, 2002.

Further Resources

Bortz, Fred. *Mind Tools: The Science of Artificial Intelligence*. New York: Franklin Watts, 1992.

Hofstader, Douglas. *Metamagical Themas: Questing for the Essence of Mind and Pattern*. New York: Basic Books. 1985.

Linden, David. *The Accidental Mind: How Brain Evolution Has Given Us Love, Memory, Dreams, and God*. Boston: Belknap Press, 2008.

Thomas, Peggy. *Artificial Intelligence*. San Diego: Lucent Books, 2005.

Web sites

Alan Turing: Computing Machinery and Intelligence

http://loebner.net/Prizef/TuringArticle.html

> *This is an online copy of one of Turing's most important scientific papers on the topic of AI, originally published in the scientific journal* Mind *in 1950. People outside the field of AI will find the advanced paper hard to understand, but it is a key part of the history of this science.*

American Association of Artificial Intelligence

http://www.aaai.org/home.html

> *This is the Web site of the leading American professional association for AI research. It includes a great deal of up-to-date information on the status of AI research and links to other resources. The "Resources for Students" section has information on careers in AI, summer camps, and doing student reports on AI.*

Forbes Magazine: The AI Report

http://www.forbes.com/2009/06/22/singularity-robots-computers-opinions-contributors-artificial-intelligence-09_land.html

> *This site includes several magazine stories about artificial intelligence.*

IBM: Deep Blue

http://www.research.ibm.com/deepblue/home/html/b.html

This site describes the first computer to beat a human world chess champion.

IBM Watson

http://www.ibm.com/watson

This is the site for Watson, the computer that competed on the quiz show Jeopardy!.

Jameco Robot Store

http://www.jameco.com/Jameco/robot/robotstore.html

This store sells kits and parts to make your own robots and other electronic devices.

Massachusetts Institute of Technology Computer Science and Artificial Intelligence Laboratory

http://www.csail.mit.edu

Learn about one of the world's leading AI research programs. This site includes news in AI research and information about MIT's AI research.

Ray Kurzweil's Accelerating Intelligence

http://www.kurzweilai.net

Kurzweil is one of the world's leading thinkers and inventors in the field of artificial intelligence.

Rochester Institute of Technology Robotics Club

http://mdrc.rit.edu

Visitors will find a robotics blog, information about the club's projects, tutorials about robotics, and more.

Stanford University: What Is Artificial Intelligence?

http://www-formal.stanford.edu/jmc/whatisai/whatisai.html

Find information on various aspects of AI on the site of one of the top computer science programs in the country.

Picture Credits

Index

About the Author

P. Andrew Karam, Ph.D., got his start in science as a sailor in the U.S. Navy's nuclear power program, where he spent eight years learning about and operating nuclear power plants on a submarine and ashore. Since leaving the Navy he has earned a Ph.D. in environmental sciences from Ohio State University and has worked as an environmental scientist and geologist, a writer, and as a radiation safety professional. He has written more than 100 technical and scientific articles, more than 100 editorials for scientific publications, and nearly 200 encyclopedia articles, in addition to more than a dozen books about science. In addition to his love of science he enjoys reading and writing, photography, traveling to new places, and learning new things with which to bore his children. He has lived in New York City since 2009.